Think for Yourself

To My Aunt Ann

I Love You So Much
For Taking The Time To
Love And Guide Me.
Not Many People Are
Blessed With Two Mothers,
But I Was.
Thank You Mom
Love

Think for Yourself

DAVID WRIGHT

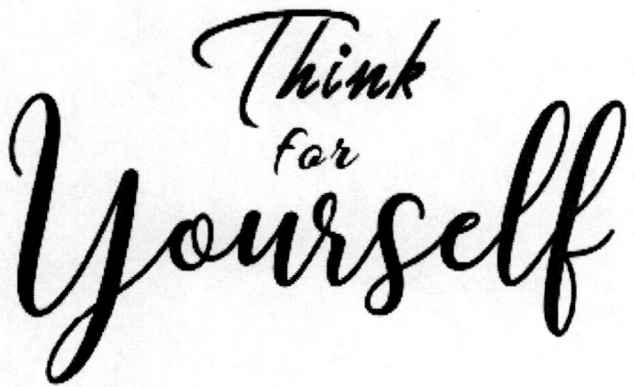

DIPS Publishing

Think for Yourself

Published by DIP'S Publishing
Cleveland, OH

www.thinkforyourself.life

ISBN: 978-1-946818-13-3

Printed in the United States of America

This book is dedicated to Robert Arthur Carter (Uncle Bobby.) Although you weren't my father, you shared with me all the wisdom and understanding that a father would share with a son. On my journey you were placed along the path. Your soul and inner peace so steadying and calming. Trust that I learned from every walk and talk that we had. I would not accept your money when offered because from you I received something of far greater value; KNOWLEDGE. When I was lost, you didn't show me the way. You taught me how to read the signs of nature so that I could find my own way; for myself. When I was drowning in anger, you didn't throw me a life preserver. You showed me the benefit of a steady and controlled spirit and taught me to swim. When I was behind in school, you didn't help me to study. You showed me how to study! And when I was hungry, you didn't give me a fish. You taught me how to use and left me to inherit rather a fishing pole. And now; I eat all I want. Thank you Uncle Bobby, for taking your time to show me what someone else showed you. With each day that I am blessed enough to rise to my feet, I promise to greet everyone as you did. Saying "Another Day, Another chance to excel, another chance to do good another chance to help somebody." My Angel, My Protector, My Mentor and My Friend; My Uncle Bobby!

TABLE OF CONTENTS

Think for Yourself

Introduction

I am so elated to be sharing this time with you. If you have purchased this book, you are a seeker just like me, and what you are seeking is seeking you.

Let this book be proof of that. I would like to say that we are friends now. Any true friend wants for you what he wants for himself. I seek mental freedom and control, and I hope you find it as well. I hope that I can help. God bless and I love you!

To Oprah Winfrey:
Thank you for being an example of positive thought.

Poem: *Along the Way*

Along the way, I have experienced every pain I have ever caused. Life is funny that way; it lets you think you've escaped, only to repay that which you owe at the most unexpected time. Along the way, I have lost many a friend, some from natural causes, some from lack of understanding. It's strange that in apparent loss, you gain the most. When things are at their worst, you receive the greatest insight. Along the way, I have wanted to give up many a time. That I didn't, I guess, is why I love me so! Everyone's along-the-way will be different; notice the scenery as you travel. Who knows if you will pass by that way again? Along the way may be rough; just make it! Make it if only to encourage another to journey! Be sincere as you can since your character is the road you will travel. Until I die, I will explore, I will roam, I will journey. I hope to see you along the way!

Romans 5:8

Those who live according to the flesh have their minds set on what the flesh desires, but those who live in accordance with the Spirit, have their minds set on what the Spirit desires. The mind governed by the flesh is death, but the mind governed by the Spirit is life and peace.

CHAPTER 1
OFFERING HELP

We have no concept of the true capacity of our minds. If I asked you about you, most likely you would start with a description of your body. You would start out with all its capabilities, but it is actually the mind that produces, manifests and brings forth all that we see. It is said that we only utilize ten percent of our brain power, but how is this possible? It is because our minds are closed. It is because we only believe what we have been told, and we only study that which we believe.

Children are free thinkers at birth, but through training, they experience a systematic wearing down of their thought process. They are first taught by parents, preachers and teachers that you must think and be like everyone else. Then they are bullied by peers and those they love into thinking that they are wrong for their free thought. Oddly enough, the people doing this, those waging verbal wars and mental assaults on our children, are the people that they trust the most. So our children are ultimately led astray and systematically convinced that their power is being provided by an external source and that they are powerless to control it.

In the chapters "Having an Open Mind" and "What If I Was Lied To?" we will explore this further. For now, let us concentrate on what we feel about our present state of mind. Do the current thoughts that you have now bring you what you find pleasing? If so, I am happy that you have found the answers. I am happy that you were taught and trained differently than most. I am happy that you instinctively understand what most have to tirelessly study to comprehend.

If you are not currently happy with your thoughts, even if just for a second, you lament what you first conceive and later achieve. Let the source help you through me to offer you an explanation for the things you have been told about you. The only difference is that the help you receive through me will be easily understood. This help provided through me will seem to take your spirit by the hand and whisper free truths you thought you would never receive. Notice that I said to be helped through me, not by me. For I am shaped just as you are; we are molded like buckets to carry the truth and to share it with others. In the chapter on apparatuses, we will discuss our purposes. For now, think of the spiritual guide, preacher, teacher or anyone who offers you help. Think of them in a way as to not lose perspective on their worth. If you can keep their worth in perspective, you will never lose sight of your own. You will never lose sight of how truly powerful you are. "This little light of mine, I'm going to let it shine!"

Think with me. Say you are on a journey in the desert and all of your supplies are lost. Now at this point, you have no way to make the journey because you are without provisions. You could make it without food because it is just a three-day journey. But without water, you are doomed; you would never survive. Now finally, you are at your end and you cannot take another step without water. Suddenly, a man comes along with a pitcher of water. You drink and you are restored. After this restoration of body and spirit, whom do you praise? More simply put, do you praise the pitcher that carried the water or do you praise the water itself for saving your life? You would praise the water itself, of course, but you would still show the proper respect to the pitcher. After all, it did play its part in your salvation. You would never for a second discard the water and only keep the pitcher; if you did, you would die. The pitcher is only good for one thing: carrying the water. YOU CANNOT DRINK THE PITCHER.

My point is this: You must show spiritual leaders love and respect for what they bring but you must also be careful not to over-respect them. The fact is, this preacher/pitcher carries water the same as you can. If you give too much credit for an everyday act like carrying water, you lose sight of your own worth. It is an everyday thing for a pitcher to carry water; it's what it was designed for. We praise the preacher so highly because he is the only one that purposely carries the water; he is the only one who has made it a point to take another's salvation seriously.

We are all pitchers. Some may be bigger and some smaller, but we all have the ability to carry water (or to carry the truth to others). Some carry a huge amount and others just a drop. If you will share that drop you have been blessed with, you can change the world. A mustard seed of faith is all that it takes to move a mountain. The mountains of doubts, fears and negative thoughts seem larger than life. The drop of water that you are worth is all it may take to nourish another and to let them drink and be restored. How will you know if your supply is enough to help if you never offer a drink to another? You are given what you need to sustain your life, but you are also given the ability to help. We are all given our share; if you have a family of ten, your share will exceed mine, but you still will just receive your share.

Your portion is decided based on your faith, not how many people you serve. You must have total faith; not faith in what you can't see, as we have been taught, but faith in what you can see: yourself. When you look into the mirror, what and who do you see? Faith in yourself requires the same amount of faith in the things you can't see, but after you believe in yourself long and strong enough, you will see that the power you praise, worship and blindly follow is the same power in you that sustains, nourishes and keeps you safe. When you have faith in things not seen and when you have faith in yourself, you are having faith in one and the same thing. When we separate the two, all your power is lost. Correction: it is given away. We must learn who we are to understand and to comprehend what we can do.

Let's discuss the thought of what we can do and what we are capable of. Let's consider a smart phone, the newest model. When we get the phone, we immediately open it up and go through the steps for activation. Once accomplished, we immediately begin use. There are very few of us who take the time to read the directions. As a result, you might have the phone for several months or even a year before you discover a hidden feature the phone possesses. But once you realize this feature, the phone takes on an aura of newness again. This aura of newness may induce you to read the manual or you may still keep using the phone blindly, impressed and pleased with this one new feature learned. Regardless, you have learned more of its abilities. You have discovered that you're only using 10 percent of the phone's capabilities. Unto your need for its abilities, will you look into it and study more. Not unto the people you serve, but unto your faith will your portion be decided. The more you understand, the more you will believe. We all know that the more you believe, the more you can do. We are capable of so much more, just like smart phones are capable of much more than just making telephone calls.

With these metaphors, I'm offering another way for you to view yourself. I am attempting to offer you this help because I know from personal experience that when we travel in ignorance, we often don't know we are one. Traveling in ignorance means that we do not know a better path than the one we are currently taking. But if you seek a way out, this thought process can help! It starts with developing, always having and keeping an open mind.

I would never hold fast to this way of thinking. If you told me that you had a better way than this, I would listen to you. I wouldn't listen to you to respond; I would listen to you to listen and to know. The difference between the two is this: When you listen to respond, you are often not listening at all. You only hear what was said up until the point you began thinking of something to say in response. After that point, you began thinking and you heard nothing because you were inside of your mind thinking of just the right words to put together in response. It's the same as daydreaming, and you can't recollect what was said. When you listen to listen, you clear your mind and just listen. You may write down a question or two, as to not forget the point you want to make, but you never take your thoughts off the person talking, and that is the only true way to listen. We don't listen that way, which is why most discussions end in argument; we only hear what we have to say. Let this new approach help you, but know that nothing about this approach is new. This is what Jesus meant when he said, "Verily, verily, I say unto you, he that believes on me, the works that I do shall he do also, and greater works than these shall he do, because I go unto my Father" (John 14:12).

Poem: *Everyone Won't Share My View*

Everyone won't share my view. I believe what I was told, that all things are possible for a true believer! However, everyone won't share my view. If my view was shared, we'd be unstoppable. If my view was shared, Christ would be believed and fear would resemble a thing of the past. Some share my view but are afraid to speak the truth. The messenger is always shot for the message. Pure thought leads to pure results, on the wings of time gliding. Some are able while others aren't. Everyone, despite outward appearance or negative past deeds done, is able to make a difference. Everyone won't share my view; some think that only some can, while some think that someone else will. They are all correct! I know that I am, and I know that you are too. But everyone won't share my view!

CHAPTER 2
CREATED IN HIS IMAGE

2 Corinthians 3:18

And we all, who with unveiled faces contemplate the Lord's glory, are being transformed into his image with ever-increasing glory, which comes from the Lord, who is the Spirit.

Where does our power come from? Whatever your belief or view, we had to come from something. How are we made in the image of the Father? I am skinny, she is heavy, he is tall and she is short; whether black, brown, white or whatever color your skin is wrapped in, how are we made the same? We are the same, because we are connected to the vine. We are just like him less one degree removed. Our one degree, our one drop of power, is expressed through our ability to think. It is that ability to think, that drop of the Father, that gives us our divinity and our dominion over the earth. It gives us our ability to commune on a higher level, to appear to read others' minds, to appear to see things before they happen. This ability is in us all; it is inherent and not earned; it is imparted in us at birth. I look at God/ the source like this: If he/it was a vast ocean, we would be drops of water. We are just like our creator; we possess the same great power. But where he is the ocean, we are only a drop of water. That drop is described or interpreted by us through the spirit. What creates us and what is on the inside of us is our spirit.

The same God, the same energy and the same spirit that makes up the power we believe we serve is in each one of us. As we serve this great all-encompassing power, and if it is learned, understood and used correctly, we could make it serve us. That may sound like blasphemy to some, but it is the great truth that Jesus lost his life trying to get others to receive.

2 Corinthians 4:7

We now have this light shining in our hearts, but we ourselves are like fragile clay jars containing this great treasure. This makes it clear that our great power is from God, not from ourselves.

The verse above describes how I see our relationship to this power after we are born. We are now and always have been a part of the whole, but when you are born, you experience the power for yourself. Think of it like this: If before being born, we were all lined up against a wall lifeless, and someone came along with an empty eye dropper. This person went to the edge of the ocean and they took the eye dropper and filled it with the Lord/the Power/the ocean and dropped a drop on top of each of our heads, which brought each of us to life. That drop is our piece of the great power that our grandparents spoke of. That drop is our ability to think, reason and to rethink. And lastly, that drop gives us our ability to apply our WILL and our DESIRE to those things we think about. That is our power of God. We have the ability to create all that we can fathom and come up with. All that you conceive and think up in your mind, all that you apply your focus on, do you not receive? All that you dwell upon, all the things that you put feeling behind and say constantly, don't they materialize in your life eventually? Not the things that you think of every now and then, but the things you think of that you just cannot let go and that either help or hurt.

Thought is your ability to make the word flesh. God said, "Let there be light," and there was light. But before God or any of us can say anything, we must have thought it first. The Bible is the biggest testament to thought ever written, because it places so much power in and on the word. The Bible places all power and all notions of power on the word. It's almost the eternal riddle—a truth that has been kept from us through the ages. But has it been kept or did we just not listen when the truth was trying to get our attention?

If money is the expression of power, then the word is the expression of thought. The word in essence is the byproduct of thought, and if that is true, all true power lies first in thought. And that is how we resemble the master. We are all one degree removed. With God being the vast ocean and us being a drop, we possess the same great power as the ocean because we are God, but just not on as grand of a scale. The power and the potentialities of its use don't start and stop within just our one drop. Because that one drop of ocean water has power to stir up and to gather unto itself other individual drops, as a single drop, we are mighty but not as mighty. As you gain the ability and the understanding to gather other drops, your strength increases. That is why we were broken up and dispersed with our speech jumbled when trying to build the temple to the sky. Our intention must always be to serve THE WHOLE.

Genesis 11:4-6

Come, let us build ourselves a city, with a tower that reaches to the heavens, so that we may make a name for ourselves; otherwise we will be scattered over the face of the whole earth.

But the LORD came down to see the city and the tower the people were building. If as one people speaking the same language they have begun to do this, then nothing they plan to do will be impossible for them.

Individually we can do little, but when two or more are gathered in his name, a lot can be accomplished, we just need to be mindful of our intent. I will give another example of how combination leads to greater results. If you take the thing that we need to survive the most and study it, you will see that what I say is true. Water is H2O; that's two parts hydrogen and one part oxygen. Brought together and joined, these elements sustain our lives. Without them joining and creating this combination that sustains our life and makes up 71 percent of the earth's surface, we would cease to exist. This goes to show the great power that can be created in combining or gathering two or more things in the name of the power. This showcases the great power in the Law of the Mastermind. That is the combining or the putting together of two or more elements. Well, my friends, man is the most precious element of all, but only if we are joined together but first taught to think properly, which would mean that the thoughts had by each of us were the thoughts that would benefit the most and not the few.

If we could conjoin and act upon those lines of thought, the world would be changed into HEAVEN overnight because the world would immediately resemble our new process of thought. Understand that what the world resembles now is only a vision internally of how we truly see it to be; this hell we experience is our thoughts being made daily into flesh.

We look externally to define how we are feeling inside. We blame what we see for making us feel the way we do, when nothing could be more false. The things you see don't dictate the way you feel. The way you feel and how you think dictates the things you see. The universe is set up in a way as to give its children divine pleasure. This earth, the world we live in and experience, is where we are to grow our Garden of Eden.

The mind is our garden, for the mind possesses the most fertile ground of all. Our thoughts are the seeds and the universe is the soil. Any thought that you plant in your WILL brings forth fruit that physically matches the mental thought; it is always equal, not lesser or greater to it. So the result of thought is always a physical manifestation; what you receive will match the thought that gave it life. And let's be clear that you can't plant an apple tree and expect oranges or grapes to grow. Simply put, thoughts of love and helpfulness will breed similar thoughts which in turn will produce circumstances in life to coincide with those thoughts. A man who thinks of all the best in the world will experience it. This is not to say that rain or any other unpleasantness will never occur in his life, but the events that happen are a mere test. It's not the situation but how you handle it that defines you.

Religion was a tool used by the creator to be a trellis to our thoughts. It helps us think along the lines of each other. Grand thoughts will reap their physical equivalent. Words are made flesh by us daily, but our power goes so unnoticed that it truly doesn't exist for our benefit. Power that goes unused is power that dissipates. If you were a poor man and you worked hard daily to save, your money would accumulate. If you hustled, scrimped and saved and managed to get a million dollars, you would be rich, right? But what if you hustled to make the first million, you kept hustling, and you kept on grinding to make the second million? Now, on this road to riches, you never spent or enjoyed your money; you just worked to get more. What if you unexpectedly died without spending any of the money? If you died without enjoying any of it, did you ever truly possess it? If you never ever used it, can you truly say that you ever really had it? Money is a lot like power in that if it goes unused, it will go away. "A fool and his money will soon part." The same is true with our divine power; we use it to bring about all our negative thoughts and all of the things we don't want. We use it to summon forth all of the things that we dwell on that could possibly go wrong in our lives.

At the end of the day, our power is regarded as a curse, not a blessing. The power that governs us leaves it up to us to choose our thoughts. Because the power adores us, it grants all that you pray for or mentally dwell upon. The thing in your mind that you see yourself doing, or possessing or going through, is the heaven or hell you summon. With the free WILL we are given, the power trusts that you will choose the best for yourself. The power does not see good and bad; it only sees what you pray for and what you mentally dwell upon. If you constantly think about losing your home, having bad health or suffering anything else that would bring you harm, pain and torment, you will receive just what you're praying/asking/begging for. Why then do you look up to a creator or creation with disdain for giving you all that you said you wanted and all that you asked for in your thoughts? It is better to praise creation for giving you what you asked for. Then immediately begin to think of only those things that will bring benefit to the world, your country, your state, your city, your neighborhood, your block, your family, your friends and finally yourself! We are where we are because we THINK HOW WE THINK!

Everything wrong in this world is blamed and falls on the next man or the government, but in truth, we possess all the power to change the rest! If we regarded the power as infinite, as it truly is, we would no longer attempt to deprive one another. It is only then that we will rise. We regard the power as weak because we don't use it for its abundance. We use it just enough to help ourselves and to help and to effect the world as much as we are able to with this limited view. As the view on this subject is narrow, only a few seem to benefit while the masses are left to die. We who understand, should help others to do so also, which will open up our view, which will allow us to understand more, which will increase thought output, which will enable us to help others more, which will enable us to benefit and receive according to our input/impact upon the whole.

Poem: *Your Lows Will Be Fewer*

Stop doubting and believe in yourself, in this process called nature, in your creator called God! Have faith in yourself like one does about tomorrow coming. You have more control over your mind than you do over the dawn of a new day. Your thoughts are why your tomorrows play out as they do. Your lows will be fewer when you understand how all are favored, how we are so pampered as to have gotten what we aspire to—all we want upon demand and command! As we desire what's undesirable, we complain to our God who says your lows will be fewer if you change your mind. Change those thoughts and let them be studied upon beforehand, so that your outcome satisfies instead of torments.

Chapter 3
What If We Were Lied To?

Ephesians 1:13

In whom ye also trusted, after that ye heard the word of truth, the gospel of your salvation: in whom also after that ye believed, ye were sealed with that Holy Spirit of promise.

We are loyal. We all love our mothers, fathers, teachers, friends and preachers. We love them because they love us. You would fight to the death to defend what you were told by one of these people. And rightly so because this person has or has had your best interest at heart for all of your life. This person, out of everyone and in spite of everyone, has always kept it real with you. These people have always genuinely cared for and made you feel safe. So when you catch a total stranger who comes speaking a truth that is different than the one you know, you take offense. You defend, you take up arms to get rid of the disrespectful intruder who would have the unmitigated gall to presume to tell us that our nanna was wrong. We totally disregard this thought, whatever it may be. Because if Nanna was wrong, not only have I been living a lie but she has also. She lied to me all these years, and I refuse to feel that she would lie to me. Liars are enemies and my NANNA is far from an enemy; she is the truth! This one thing we tend to forget.

We put so much faith, so much belief and so much of ourselves into these people that we forget one thing: I am made in his image as we all are. He made me knowing my destiny before a breath was taken. If I am, as we all are, in his image made, and if I can be lied to by someone who loves me, then so can they! They could have been lied to, misled or misguided the same as I am now. What if the philosophy preached, taught and engrained into the minds of our loved ones, to later be instilled into us, was a lie?

We regard a lie as a harsh thing. But everything done in the moment by each of us is perfect. The lie that was told to you was one that was told to them by someone they trusted. And so on and so forth it goes back to the beginning of time. But was it really a lie, or was it simply a misinterpretation? When we were children and the teacher told a secret to the first person in the first row in front of the class, the secret was whispered to each student, and by the time it had made it to the back, it was a totally different secret than the one that had been started. But it was told by the second to last person to the person next to him as the unmitigated truth just as it was with the second in line to the first person who ever told it.

In life, you very seldom have a chance to go back to the original source and find out exactly what was said. The lie that has been precipitated by saint and sinner alike is the lie that separates us all. It is the lie that has been told to steal or to induce us to give away our true power: the power of thought. This power is taken, or rather freely given away, the second you close your mind. A closed mind is one that only harbors and adheres to one view above all others. It is a mind that rejects a new point of view without even hearing it first.

If you ever have been told a lie and wanted to be blessed with the truth, an open mind is the only way you will receive truth. The truth is said to have the power to set one free. With the truth you have been told, and currently feel, live and breathe, how free do you really feel? The truth you and I have been told is that God is up and we are down. That he is inside and we are outside. This is all a lie! God your father is as inside of you as is the blood that pumps in your veins.

Of course you are beaten and of course you are defeated because you don't know this truth. Some call it God, some call it the spirit and others call it the philosophy of the mind. You are all correct, so none should, can or will be excluded from its power. The power we serve is the power of thought. It's the power you serve or the power you employ to serve you. You think every year of every month of every day of every hour of every minute of every second, whether you are conscious or not, sleep or awake. The act or the art of thinking still takes place. Your heart and lungs operate on the same system. But your thought differs because it follows a definite pattern. Now your thought operates automatically, but you set it in motion by an initial thought. Once set in motion, it continues to have thoughts similar to the original. Now thoughts are things; your thoughts are your God power and your ability to create, to make words flesh. God said, "Let there be light," and there was light. You said, "I need a better job," and you got one. Or you said, "I'm going to get fired," and you were. Your thoughts follow themselves as if trained. One thought breeds and leads another thought and another and another until you can touch the result.

As you have these thoughts, they produce into your life with mathematical timing and precision according to your faith and according to your belief of what you think will happen. This is what is meant by the verse that says it only takes the faith of a mustard seed to move a mountain.

If my mother would have had the truth explained to her this way, I know she would have told me what I now say to you. Yes, we were lied to by the ones who loved us, but only because they didn't know any better. They thought they told us the truth, so no disrespect can be leveled. If from what you were taught you have no questions, your life is perfect and you should throw this book in the trash. But if you have any questions, if now your spirit reaches out to learn to eat of the truth, then feed it with this book. Open the mind of your family, your children, those you love and even those you don't to this great power.

The truth is this: We were lied to but we can stop the lies and begin telling the truth. It all starts with us. Will you tell the truth or keep spreading the lies? From this day forth, facilitating the truth is all up to you! What will you do? Even if you don't believe, others at least have the right to know. They have the right to know so they can choose which path to follow. The only thing needed to get down to the bottom of anything is WILL and a thought. We set such a powerful force in motion when we employ the two. The logic of it all is this: The way that we think now has war, perversions, hate and poverty running rampant. The way we have been trained and led to believe keeps the masses poor and a few wealthy. How can that be the truth that a divine, higher power would level at any of us? Only slavery would ask this of the people involved in its process. Only slavery would ask the masses to suffer so that a few could benefit. That is a thought precipitated and followed on our own that has us doing such.

The power wants us to have and to share in all the abundance it has to offer. We were taught the total opposite. Will this be enough to endure? You want to think about another way that says I AM, and with the knowledge of that, all things are possible. All I need is an understanding of myself to be able to utilize power and knowledge that dates back to dates. It says that I am able and fortified with the power of thought to do all things. I am here to tell you that we were lied to; I can only hope that you receive the truth and are set free from limitations, from lack, and most importantly, from yourself.

Poem: *Elevate Your Highest Thought*

What is your highest thought? Stop; raise it by 10. It is your current way of thinking that has you in your present condition. If you are pleased, by all means stay the same. But...for even a second if you are not, elevate your highest thought. Think those lofty thoughts that will bring you pleasure and not difficulties you don't choose to endure. Let your highest thought carry you over the humps of mundaneness and mediocrity into the heavens of your reality. A man can only rise as high as his highest thought. What's your highest thought? Stop and raise it by ten. It is your current way of thinking that has you where you are. If not satisfied, train your mind on that thing that seems out of reach. Aspire to be great, and you will obtain. Always shoot for the moon. If you miss, you are still amongst the stars! You must only... elevate your highest thought!

Chapter 4

Have an Open Mind to Receive

Acts 17:11

Now the Berean Jews were of more noble character than those in Thessalonica, for they received the message with great eagerness and examined the Scriptures every day to see if what Paul said was true.

True knowledge is just out of the scope of what we know; it is on the north side of STUDY. We must push our boundaries of understanding. We are connected. If true, what is unbelievable, unachievable and unobtainable? Nothing; all is possible. The truth has always been in front of us. Every saying that is heard is meant in one way or another to help us understand the truth. Watch what you wish for; you just might get it. That's a saying used to warn you about how powerful your mental abilities are. Another saying is, "You get what you give/you reap what you sow." That is to explain and express that we are part of the vine; we are connected to each other. When you hurt, offend or even think an ill thought about another, you're only doing it to yourself! When Jesus said, "What you do to the least of my people, you do unto me," he was saying what you do to others, you do unto yourself!

You need an open mind to realize your true abilities. We are ALL made incredible, but you can only begin to believe that with an open mind. Once your mind is open, you begin to truly achieve. With an open mind, you finally begin to conceive. High thought breeds higher thought; nature calls this evolution. The Bible calls it all things working for the greater good for those who believe. Show a non-believer how to believe by believing yourself, not by force. Instead of helping each other to understand, we attempt to force each other to assimilate to what we believe instead of having an open mind. An open mind lets you come to a version of the truth that you are comfortable with, a version in which all questions are answered and explained. A closed mind only allows you to experience similar sorrows, pains and joys experienced by those you precede and those who think like you. No new thing can you experience, less by chance. If you think the same things that you have always thought, you will get the very same things that you have always received. Like in the stock market crash, when all the old ways failed, it forced the minds of men to come up with new ways to achieve. So it is in nature when something is destroyed: something better arises from the ashes, like a phoenix. On the other side of failure is always triumph. It's always darkest before the dawn. Be optimistic; let your views remain open until you have found the right one, and always and forever expand upon it.

The truth is living, breathing and always expanding. The truth evolves the same as evolution does, so subsequently, today's truth just might not fit yesterday's description of it. Expand upon what you know. Any nurse, any computer programmer, and any physician must take continuing education classes to keep up with the times as they change. Yes, amazing as it may seem, times they do change. Our thoughts must change, elevate and grow to keep up with them. Anyone who tells you that truth doesn't change is mistaken. He is mistaken because he repeats what he has been told or what has been studied by those he was trained by.

It is not disrespectful to change what you believe. We are not wrong; we are right. I think therefore I am. Because thought never stops, we think even in slumber. The mind always works. In sleep, the mind follows the grooves and patterns of the thoughts had in the day. It completes the processes unable to be finished by either lack of understanding or lack of energy. When you slumber, your subconscious takes over and instinctively finishes all you could not. Your subconscious works like your heart and lungs, but with one difference: it thinks as you command it to. It follows your thought process to know what you want. Your thought process is the actual blueprint of the subconscious. Change what you are thinking and keep your mind open to the possibilities that will now surely present themselves, because what you are seeking is seeking you. To keep an open mind is to have faith. "Faith is the confidence that what we hope for will actually happen; it gives us assurance about things we cannot see."

An open mind is needed to learn, to continue to learn and to understand your thoughts. And after this is done, an open mind is needed to explore all the possibilities and all the combinations that are possible to help and to impact the whole. If you want to truly be selfish and look out for yourself in the ultimate way, give to others that which you most want yourself, and treat other people how you want to be treated yourself. That is the only way to bring the continuous results in your life that you need, desire and require! It is impossible to think separation without being separated. If you think in terms of cheating your brother, your brothers will think in terms of cheating you. If you give love, you will receive love. By our thoughts, we are able to line up our daily experiences. If you think in terms of giving and love, you will walk in those terms as well. The terms that you walk in, you will experience. Understand that fact, because that is truly the reality you live in now. You are living a reality precipitated by your thought. If the reality that you live isn't all that you want it to be, all you must do to change it is to change the way you think. It won't happen overnight, but at the end of it, the process will seem like it did happen in the blink of an eye.

Once you change your thoughts to coincide with the future you truly desire, your life will change. It will change into that which you wish. When you open your mind, you will receive, but you'll also begin to notice in life the beauty that is taking place in your mind. Pleasant thoughts breed more than opportunities. They breed beauty! You will begin to notice the nature around you. You will begin to notice all the beauty in the world that has lined up with your thoughts. We live in the matrix, except you are the only programmer at the wheel. What is sent to you is only everything you ask, desire and need for help. Keep an open mind so that you can learn to use all of your mental ability. If you are skeptical, remember that people will often deprive you of power or cheat you out of it. But not many people point power out and seek to explain to you how to use it.

If I found a million dollars, I wouldn't seek to hide it and keep it for myself. Instead, I would divide it up and pass out everyone's share; then I would give investment classes. There is no greater gift a person can give than to attempt to enlighten another. If you give a man a fish, he will eat for a day, but if you teach a man to fish, he will eat for a lifetime. Now that you have been told how to fish, it is your duty to pass on your knowledge.

Each one should do his very best to teach one. Our thoughts breed power. All of us have been given just enough to sustain only ourselves. Let us open our minds so that we can gain. Let us open our minds so that we can receive. Let us open our minds so that we can help. Notice that gain and receive were first on the agenda. The power knows that we seek these things. It wants to give us everything we want and at the same time help everyone else. This is a beautiful way of doing things if you give it proper thought. Because of the way we are made, you receive the physical equivalent of your thought. All we must do to succeed is to get on the right page with creation. We must align our thoughts up with those lofty thoughts. If you pray for a million dollars, pray for ten million; that will be enough for everyone else as well as yourself. Make your plans grand enough to include others; that's lofty thought. Change your mind from being closed to charity to being open to it. When you open your mind up to giving, the only charity case you help is yourself. Help to heal others' broken hearts and spirits so that yours too can be made whole.

God is love, only because that is the purest emotion. With love guiding all of your other thoughts, feelings and emotions, you will succeed. You will bring into play that reality that would seek to have you taking full advantage of your gifts. Don't merely try to "keep your head above water," because then after you exert all the efforts you have, you are still just a step above drowning. Stop saying and thinking what you do not want. Open your mind up to the fact that "as a man thinketh, so shall he be." Stop blaming God for your life. You can't blame God for your life because he didn't have your thoughts. He in his infinite wisdom gave you the power to think, but he also gave us free will. He did this so no one could control our minds. Truly understand this: If you have a closed mind, you let another with an open mind control yours. This is simply explained by the force that is always moving. If you don't move, nature will get something going that will make you move. Once something else forces you to move, that something has the control. Open your mind, so that you and only you can begin controlling you!

Poem: *"Who Art Thou?" God Asked*

For I am man put here to serve you—a galaxy all to himself! I am the smile on God's face; I am his ability to show emotion to the world. Through me, your beauty gets and is expressed. Most times I falter from my duties because I have fallen out of touch with you, and my connection to the vine broken. It takes much self-recognition and courage to know that you are the expression of the father. We are no longer his smile; we have fallen to the level of admirer. Thanks-giver only, not the children of the almighty. His children would never fear; his children would never hate. His children would be too busy planning courageously and executing fearlessly, expressing all the beauty in nature that God has placed inside each of us but with a twist: besides possessing great beauty, we also have a voice to describe and to articulate all that is seen! Imagine a beautiful garden that can talk. “Who art thou?” God asked, and I replied, “I am the son of a king and the child of the Almighty!”

Chapter 5
My WILL/My Connection

1 Corinthians 14:24-25

But if an unbeliever or an inquirer comes in while everyone is prophesying, they are convicted of sin and are brought under judgment by all, as the secrets of their hearts are laid bare. So they will fall down and worship God, exclaiming, "God is really among you!"

You must know where you have been to know where you are going. Where you have been is who you are. Where you have been relies on what you are a part of. What you are a part of depends on what you are connected to. Who made you? Why were you made? What came first: the chicken or the egg?

We are all perfect in the moment, one degree removed. Our carnage takes time to develop. Free will, no matter what is done, leads to the expansion and elevation of mankind. ALL THINGS WORK FOR THE GREATER GOOD FOR THOSE THAT BELIEVE. If this be true, what does this mean? If all work the greater good no matter what, by definition all things done by believers/thinkers are perfect. ALL THINGS WORK FOR THE GREATER GOOD FOR THOSE THAT BELIEVE. If the truth is absolute, and we all know it to be, then the things done by anyone are for the greater good.

This lends so much to the expression of being connected. We are connected in such a way that we can›t fail. All things work for the greater good. How much good will you do? Your WILL determines your way. Your way is the thoughts you have, and the thoughts you have make up the life that you live and encounter. As a man thinketh, so shall he be. The Bible sheds light on thought, which is your WILL, all throughout it. You can›t serve two masters. WHAT YOU LIKE YOU WILL WANT, WHAT YOU WANT YOU WILL THINK ABOUT AND WHAT YOU THINK ABOUT, YOU WILL GET. So what is your WILL?

What you want is not simply what you say you want. It is that thing you most concentrate and focus on; that is your WILL. And your WILL will be done on earth as it is in heaven. But it›s truly in heaven (in the mind through thought) as it is on earth (what you can see before you physically; what you can hold and touch). Your WILL must be used to benefit the whole, not to antagonize it. Your WILL must be used to add to it, not to take away. That is the only way you can achieve your perfection. Because as you give, you shall receive. Give what? Your time, your body and your thought. Receive what? EVERYTHING AND MORE!

Luke 6:38–"Give, and it shall be given unto you; good measure, pressed down, and shaken together, and running over, shall men give into your bosom. For with the same measure that ye mete withal it shall be measured to you again."

Give; it will not be done in vain. When you tithe, you say to the universe, "I believe; I give that which I wish to receive." We will all need something different, but if you give, you will get. Tithing helps you to remember that. Religion and philosophy are only a way to help keep your thoughts straight. They are but mere examples of life. You must live your life and identify with the messages, stories and sayings to find your way, to see how these things apply and relate to your life. They are blueprints to navigate your days. You must live to see what applies to you. Not everything will, but there is no situation invented that it does not display how to use your thought abilities to achieve.

Your WILL is shaped by your thought. How you use your abilities is entirely up to your understanding of them. As your understanding rises, so will your thoughts and in turn your WILL will be as strong as the will it took to say, "LET THERE BE LIGHT." Our WILL has the power to change the world. There is evidence of this by the world we see, for it was shaped, molded and made by the thoughts in which we are having now. What we see today in our lives is but the reflection of what we thought and saw ourselves yesterday. What we will eventually become tomorrow is a result of the thoughts that we are having and the way that we see ourselves today. Will you build your tomorrows out of hay, out of straw or out of brick? Which little pig are you? The hay resembles negative thoughts that say you will lose, you aren›t good enough and you have no place. The straw pieces are those words such as "I'M BROKE" or "I CANT" or "This is TOO DIFFICULT." Those thoughts make you weak.

Words of brick and solid foundation are the thoughts, phrases and words like-"SMALL THING TO A GIANT" and "IF I CAN CONCEIVE, I CAN ACHIEVE!" These thoughts are the reasons for your yesterdays, the causes of your todays and the shape of your tomorrows. What do you think about yourself? Now is the time to begin to rebuild your tomorrows, regardless of what today was like. Change your thoughts of yourself; what do you have to lose? If I am wrong, what will you give up by following me? The only thing you will stop doing to yourself by listening to me is condemning yourself. You judge yourself harshly, and all these judgments are how you see yourself. I say that you are beautiful, unordinary and awesome. I say this statement and all these words with the greatest sincerity. I say you are beautiful, unordinary and awesome because I am as well. We are all made in his image. So if I be, you are also! YOU ARE WHAT YOU WILL YOURSELF TO BE. You have the ability to be all you can.

We suffer because we don›t understand. Think of yourself in terms of a blessing, so that you can be one. Open your mind so that you can receive all that you can become. Claim the greatness that you are destined for. Your mind can only become that which you see. Look to see more so you can be more. The more you are, the more others will see. If by my thoughts, I raise you, and if by your thoughts, you raise another, won›t all our thoughts be ELEVATED? Your thoughts make up you, so for you to keep an open mind means you grow. An open mind means that you are growing constantly. It means you are exploring your mind and all it has to offer.

Education is not the only way to receive enlightenment. We are part of an energy force that knows all, and an open mind can access all the universe has to offer. An open mind opens your sail of thought and places the winds of the universe at your back. It gives you the heart to pursue and the backbone not to quit. On this journey, so much comes because we are not in control. Peace be still, and become the captain of your ship. Notice your power and reclaim it; build yourself through thought. As sons of the father, we are capable and able, but you are only as able as you know you are and as you give yourself credit for being. Open your mind and guide others to liberty.

Harriet Tubman freed the slaves. It will take each one of us to help free the slaves of our mentalities. We are doomed to repeat these tired days if we don›t change our thoughts. Let change be precipitated by you. You can start change by simply inspiring thought. Give of yourself so that you can be given to. Open your heart to receive love. If you keep filling your mind with hate and the things you don›t want, you will keep receiving those things. Be open-minded enough to see that that›s what›s happening. If you understand this, you will stop blaming God and instead blame yourself. SIMPLY CHANGE WHAT YOU ARE THINKING AND LIVE IN BLISS!

We have the power of God inside of us; all we need to do is to control our thoughts. The guideline for controlling your thoughts is living by the Golden Rule: "Do unto others as you would have them do unto you." This sounds so trivial, but it takes an elevated mind to attempt to be to others what you would have them be to you. This state of mind takes training and effort. Every mental push-up you do in this direction will strengthen your thought power by leaps and bounds.

There is nothing like getting and keeping a feeling of inspiration. When you train yourself to think lofty, my brothers and sisters, you will be all the inspiration you need. You will be able to motivate yourself.

This truth and power is real, only it must be harnessed and controlled. With the power of thought, you can kill, steal and destroy. But you can also love, uplift and create. One power is the power that is in you and the other power is in the world. WHICH MASTER/SCHOOL OF THOUGHT WILL YOU CHOOSE TO SERVE?

Poem: *Every Drop of Rain Has a Job to Do*

Nothing happens by chance; every drop of rain that falls has a job to do. Each has its destination, its purpose. Each will nourish life in some way. The drops that fall on concrete seep somewhere giving birth to something, while sustaining something else. Much like the rain are we, all given a purpose to fulfill. Some of us know our assignments; they are those drops that fall on beautiful flowers. Their value and worth is easily seen. Others of us fall on asphalt. Since no worthwhile thing has attracted us, we feel unneeded and forgotten. But it is that rose underneath the slab of concrete that we give life to and nourish. Every raindrop has a job to do whether evident or hidden. We seek to learn and to understand, to rise and to uplift, because we all have a job to do!

CHAPTER 6

WHAT KIND OF APPARATUS AM I?

Ezekiel 44:5

The LORD said to me, "Son of man, look carefully, listen closely and give attention to everything I tell you concerning all the regulations and instructions regarding the temple of the LORD. Give attention to the entrance to the temple and all the exits of the sanctuary."

I am a machine and my level of understanding determines my output. My level of faith in what I understand is my battery pack. I can only achieve what I can conceive. You can only conceive what you deem possible and what you can understand. Some things you hear are absurd. Years down the line, you find yourself incorporating that thing into your life when you understand its true intent and purpose. Be careful what you disregard out of lack of understanding. Open-mindedness attracts the unknown: knowledge. Close-mindedness repels it.

Then he touched their eyes saying, "According to your faith be it unto you" (Matthew 9:29). So what does "we are an apparatus" mean? An apparatus is the technical equipment needed for a particular activity or purpose. We are the machinery and the purpose is the advancement of the kingdom!

Unto your faith, you will be able to express your power and to display the dominion you have over all that you see. Dominion is granted by the power you have to shape the world, the atoms in it and even the matter that makes up everything you see by the power of thought.

Again, what is your highest thought? You are only able to rise as high as your highest thought. Your faith is always along the same lines as your thoughts; you only believe what you can conceive. If you don't understand something, if you can't wrap your mind around that thing you discuss, then it is disregarded. But if you can increase your faith and your level of belief, you will be able to increase your output of expression and your output of power. You can clearly see where the power displayed is regulated by understanding and understanding only.

Power comes from our ability to apply universal law to our lives, and it is a byproduct of our level of understanding. Power in the metaphysical world can be equated to money. Understanding and your ability to apply the law in the spiritual world is the same as mastering your job in the physical world and receiving currency. Understanding and money are both expressions of power. One is merely in the world you can't see and the other is in the world you can see. To increase your level of money earned, you work harder; to increase your level of understanding, you need only to think to achieve.

Luke 8:17

For nothing is secret, that shall not be made manifest; neither anything hid, that shall not be known and come abroad.

What you seek seeks you. That's the power of your thoughts. What you seek is what you think about, so you think about what you attract. Watch what you wish for; you just might get it. Let us use our power to show that we understand.

Your power and your abilities will increase as your understanding increases. Making a difference is making the world a better place through your efforts. Mr. Carnegie, Mr. Ford, Mr. Gates and all the other giants of industry are only giants because of the level of impact they have had. These individuals have given the world so much, but there is still more to be given. Do you think the world will stop evolving? It never will because its nature is to evolve! The only thing that remains constant is the power of thought, and in that statement you can clearly see why "He will never leave nor forsake you," because it is impossible for the power to leave or fail.

Our mind continuously works; it continuously thinks. Again, HE WILL NEVER LEAVE NOR FORSAKE YOU! Raise your level of faith so you can do more in the process of expansion. All things work for the greater good, but let your thoughts be had and not stumbled upon. Begin to think diligently to inspire and to motivate change. The faith of a mustard seed of thought can move mountains. What can the faith the size of a mountain do? You are a machine designed and created for the expansion of the universe, and since God doesn't make junk, what are you good for?

Do you have the faith that it takes to believe in the power of your words to bless? Or do you disregard your power of the word? Do you use your words to curse? We are vessels designed to carry the way, the truth and the light. Sometimes we find ourselves carrying, passing on and flat out embodying negativity, lies and darkness. No man can find his way to the kingdom of his mind (heaven) if in himself he regards those thoughts. As you do unto others, you do unto yourself! If you think hellish thoughts for another, it is you through the power of thought that lives their hell already in your mind. "As a man thinketh, so shall he be." It is up to us to give, first of our minds and then of ourselves. That is the only true path. You must first think in order to do. All we need to do is to put our best foot forward in thought.

Think before you speak. Once something is said, it belongs to the past and can never be taken back. However, thoughts can be retrieved; all you need to do is repent on that thought and ask forgiveness.

Acts 13:39, therefore, my friends, I want you to know that through Jesus the forgiveness of sins is proclaimed to you.

A sin is the thought of something that is contrary to your growth. You sin when you harbor ill feelings towards another, because anything you do against the whole, you really do to yourself. Sooner or later that pain you inflict is a feeling you will have to endure! We must seek to help and to be a blessing. Explore your mind as to uncover your talents. We are given great abilities, but be careful not to waste them!

Luke 19:20-26

Then another servant came and said, "Sir, here is your mina; I have kept it laid away in a piece of cloth. I was afraid of you, because you are a hard man. You take out what you did not put in and reap what you did not sow."

His master replied, "I will judge you by your own words, you wicked servant! You knew, did you, that I am a hard man, taking out what I did not put in, and reaping what I did not sow? Why then didn't you put my money on deposit, so that when I came back, I could have collected it with interest?"

Then he said to those standing by, "Take his mina away from him and give it to the one who has ten minas."

"Sir," they said, "he already has ten!"

He replied, "I tell you that to everyone who has, more will be given, but as for the one who has nothing, even what they have will be taken away."

Poem: *Give It*

I can give you the secret to life in two words: GIVE IT. What is meant by this? Give what and to whom? I will explain for anyone who is willing to listen. I say that we are brothers and sisters in the body of spirit that represents this whole we call creation. Everything you see and everything that is, you are a part of. You are connected as sure as the grape at the end of the orchard is connected to the very first grape at the beginning of the vine! If you poison the last, will you not affect the first? If you feed and water the first, will you not be helping the last?

The hate you give or punch is directed at the last grape but it only impacts the first, which is you. If you would be in need of help, give it to that man you see withering in front of you. You need only to keep living to receive that same nourishment through the vine back to yourself! The smart person would feed and give nourishment to all he could. Instead of hitting another, assault yourself and do away with the middle man. That kind act or love you constantly bestow, remember that you will never go without. Do unto others as you would have them to do unto you! Give that which you wish to receive, and you will always HAVE!

Chapter 7
It Is Good to Be Selfish

Matthew 6:4

But when you give to the needy, do not let your left hand know what your right hand is doing, so that your giving may be in secret. Then your Father, who sees what is done in secret, will reward you.

If one reaps what they sew, then it would stand to reason that if consciously you give, you will receive. It is proven that it takes thought to do anything. If you continuously give, you set up thoughts of giving. After time, a practice becomes a habit. As you habitually give, you will eventually habitually receive. This is the law of reciprocation and it is perfectly natural to want to return a gift. Give to a friend and see if they give in return. The same is true for nature and the universe. Give unto them and they will give unto you. If you know this and you are not giving, you are a fool. That which you give you receive. To stay in reception you must stay in service. If you stay in service, you are selfish because you know that all you bestow on another you will receive. So all that you lavish on the poor, your family or a friend and stranger alike, you really give to yourself. The blessings you store in the kingdom of heaven are the blessings of thought. The kingdom is your mind, which is the only place that a heaven and a hell could ever truly exist. If you think a certain way, that is also how you will live. A tree bears fruit unto its kind. If you give, you will always receive.

How do you get what you want? The only way to get what you want is to give it. So to GET, you must GIVE; to be BLESSED, you must be a BLESSING. If to get, you know you must give and you desire to get. Then it must be your will to GIVE, GIVE, GIVE because it is your will to GET, GET, GET.

Psalms 23:5

You anoint my head with oil, my cup runneth over.

A righteous man is righteous in thought first. That is the true yin and yang, the pull of the universe—the law of diminishing return. YOU GET WHAT YOU GIVE. Every illegitimate act we commit is proof and testament to the fact that we now don't care. It is not that we don't care on purpose. It is that the message of caring has been distorted so much that in our lack of caring for others, we think we are caring for ourselves, but this couldn't be further from the truth. When you inflict pain, you must first think pain. Any thought you entertain is thought you attract, and any thought you attract will be a thought you endure, first mentally and then physically. Thoughts are things, so now you can understand what was meant when Jesus said, "What you do to the least of my brothers you do unto me." We must be honest and fair with each other if we want others to be honest and fair with us.

If we watch what we think and only think according to the whole, it will be habit to think correctly. Once that is done, you will have no problem being selfish. Once you find yourself in the bosom of this splendor, it will be impossible to leave. One thought to help will breed another and another; it will keep attracting that unto it's kind until all the love you lavish on other, the universe begins to lavish on you. If I give for a period of time, my giving will increase. When I find myself loving to give to others, I will then find the universe loving to give to me. But the more I give to others, the more I inspire the thoughts of what we need to live. If I am giving and others are receiving, they too will give so that other can receive.

This cycle of life is so apparent because we live the opposite at this moment. It is never thought that all we live in our day-to-day lives is all that we go through daily in our minds. We must be selfish and give only that which we want. If you don't care about others, that's fine. Only give because you know you will receive; it matters not. The outcome is the same. You must give with a loving heart or your gift won't be regarded. If you give with malice in your heart, you couldn't be giving your best gift. When you give your best, you are more than happy to do it. When you give your best, you live to see the expression on another's face. It is good to be selfish in this way because it inspires the absolute best thought going out into creation.

Ecclesiastes11:1-2

Ship your grain across the sea; after many days you may receive a return. Invest in seven ventures, yes, in eight; you do not know what disaster may come upon the land.

Give so that you can be sure you receive. If you give not, you will receive not, and if you don't receive, how will you live?

If you don't give, you won't receive naturally. If you don't receive naturally, you will survive by taking. After all, you must receive in order to live. But living by taking isn't living at all; it is just a means to survive. It is just a way to exist. You only live when you receive your supply naturally. You only exist and survive when you receive it synthetically. The difference between the two is this: A natural supply can be counted upon, like a farmer counts upon his crop. A synthetic supply cannot be counted upon. It is dependent on other variables to play their part.

If you rely on your supply and your supply comes only from taking from others, what happens when none are around and you are in need? Or what happens when you have taken all that can be given from those around you? The result is the same; your supply is depleted. You can never deplete a natural supply without another taking its place. Our problem is that we worry needlessly. We are connected to the source, just as any living thing on this planet. To be honest, I have never seen a tree or a flower or a rabbit or a duck worry. They carry on and persevere through any hardship, but they place no concern on supply. They are confident in the fact that all will be provided for them. They possess a faith, an instinct that we do not. What they possess in faith, we embrace in fear. All we have to do to receive is to give. We are clear in the ways it takes to lose. Now let us embody the spirit it takes to win. We must be selfish and give to another all we hope one day to receive! We must give without expecting them to repay.

We must receive our bounty from the Source. If we receive our bounty from the Source, it is everlasting. If we receive our sustenance from the world, it will dry up! Because in living in the flesh, you are as only as good as the last thing you have done. When living in the spirit, YOU ARE GRANTED GRACE!

Luke 14:12

Then Jesus said to his host, "When you give a luncheon or dinner, do not invite your friends, your brothers or sisters, your relatives, or your rich neighbors; if you do, they may invite you back and so you will be repaid. But when you give a banquet, invite the poor, the crippled, the lame, the blind, and you will be blessed. Although they cannot repay you, you will be repaid at the resurrection of the righteous."

Poem: *Both Sides*

My flesh says yes and my thoughts say no.
Who shall I follow behind on life's rides?
I will take the time out to look at it now objectively from both sides.
I feel my spirit up rising deep down inside me wanting to do something real.
In comes my flesh and along comes the test; will I do what's right or that which I feel?
Feeling feels good; let none of us lie because this truth is a fact,
Although good feelings can lead to bad decisions/result/a taskmaster for life whipping your back.
Joy and pain go hand in hand not true for when you scientifically think.
You are given dominion over the lesser creatures as long as your intentions spiritual requirements they meet.
In flesh we hit and miss uncertain of love and what the word omnipotence means.
Omnipresent is love in the spiritual realm so the decision is clear for me.
For those to still unsure, let's continue for you because we are all one in the same.
The weakest one of us must be given that strength because he's the linchpin of the chain.
My thoughts say no; now my body says no. I have chosen to which I will ride.
Now it's your turn to objectively think and look at it from both sides.

Chapter 8

There Is No Good/ There Is No Bad

1 Chronicles 28:9

And you, my son Solomon, acknowledge the God of your father, and serve him with wholehearted devotion and with a willing mind, for the LORD searches every heart and understands every desire and every thought. If you seek him, he will be found by you; but if you forsake him, he will reject you forever.

God said, "Let there be light," and there was light. The word light was inspired by the thought of illumination. What followed is a thing that we call the sun. There is no good and there is no bad, only thought.

Luke 6:37

Do not judge, and you will not be judged. Do not condemn, and you will not be condemned. Forgive, and you will be forgiven.

In the moment, all is perfect. We do that which we think is right. We are one and we are all alike. Hindsight is 20/20. In the moment, all actions taken are perfect to each of us. The end result will let you know if the intent of what you did was for the greater good or for personal gain. The greater good perseveres and becomes; it lives and breathes.

That which isn't for the greater good appears to have life, but it only has energy. This energy will inevitably dissipate. Life lives; it never fizzles out. Even when it dies, it is recycled into a newer interpretation of life. So there is no good or bad, only thought.

All things are done in order to achieve, to produce and to initiate/precipitate another action and another thought. In the mind of the doer, all seems to be a worthy and worthwhile action, because none among us plans to fail. We all live in the moment, and whatever decision was made at the time for the individual at that moment in their minds was the best thing to be done for them. The woman who drowns her children in the tub did so because in her mind she was saving them from the world or whatever she saw as harmful, hurtful and destructive. This is no different than what any other mother would do in the sense of protecting her children from being harmed, from being hurt and from being destroyed. Another mother surely would have picked another way, a way that would have spared life. But to judge this mother that killed her children, is to judge yourself by saying you don't make mistakes and that all your thoughts are for the greater good of the whole.

Everyone will have to answer for their shortcomings, but it certainly shouldn't be to each other. Most of us don't possess the skills to decipher and to discern the word of truth enough for even a child to understand. So how can WE presume to sit in the judgement seat and to pass judgement for any reason or for anything against another?

If we stop regarding bad and good, we will stop judging. If we stop judging, we will be able to commune with each other on a higher level, and if we are able to commune with each other on this higher level, we will eventually come back together as one. We will not be the Black race, the Brown race, the White race or the Yellow race; we will be the human race, which is not a race at all but a marathon that will take all the stamina in the world to complete! It is a marathon because our life, our existence and our presence on this planet is truly a never-ending story. It has been growing, changing and evolving since the dawn of man. Cars once amazed us but now a spaceship and satellites are common! Nothing is good or bad because everything done since the beginning of time has led us to this point where we are right now. If anything was changed, we would not be living in this age of modern marvels.

Some sit on the side steeped in misery looking at the world as the inspiration for their unhappiness. When in truth, you poison yourself as well as the world with your sick thoughts! Your thoughts are sick because they aren't beneficial to the whole; they aren't even beneficial to yourself. As all things work for the greater good, mankind will benefit from your thoughts. How is it just that we benefit and you as an individual, you do not? It isn't fair, by no means, but the unfairness you experience in life is precipitated by your thought and by your thought alone! There is no good and there is no bad; there is only thought.

After the thought or after the fact, all is left to interpretation by onlookers. Think as we will, but the individual is and can be the only one to want to change his thoughts. But by him doing so, he also (as thoughts are things) changes his actions. As we know better, we will instinctively think better, and all actions will follow. If we regard nothing as good and evil, our level of understanding will increase. We will stop judging and looking at that thing you did and put more of our focus and attention on what made you do it.

If you had three children and a wife, and you lost your job a month ago, there is nothing about you that is lazy. Today is Sunday and it marks the end of the month. Now for the last 26 days (not counting Sundays), you have been putting in job applications. Well, today is Sunday; you have no money and no food at home. You feel less than a man as you watch your family go hungry. Regardless of how, you get up and go out to find food for them. With no money in hand, you go into the grocery store, you steal and get caught. Everyone who looks on presumes that you are a thief—a lazy man who would rather steal than go to work. But, you and I both know that nothing could be further from the truth! We must stop judging people's intent because it is what we don't know and couldn't possibly understand. We must look to understand another's reasoning behind their thoughts. If we would only look to perceive the why, as opposed to the what, it would mean much. If we did this, we would see that maybe our thoughts of perfection or liberty or survival don't differ as much as we think. Don't offer judgement; offer help.

We are not so different. We all want to win and to be recognized and to be loved. Notice that and you will not treat and judge others so harshly. If you stop judging and step back, you may see a little piece of yourself in them. Since we all are created from the same, trust me when I say that you indeed see a bit of yourself in them. A bit of you is in all you see and a bit of all you see is in you! There is no good and there is no bad; there is only evolution, progress and growth. Everything done, said and thought, no matter what it is, contributes to that end result. So everything thought, done and said should be regarded, watched and controlled.

Since none of us are fools, we should all be living and experiencing everything that the world has to offer. Our actions facilitate growth, and at the least, they should also facilitate our individual happiness. I love you and I am happy; why shouldn't you be? I am happy with myself because I AM happy with and I love my thoughts. I am at home inside my mind. Inside my mind, I don't fear, I don't despair, I don't regret. Inside my mind, I feel safe; I am never rushed. Inside my mind, I see myself doing all that I could have ever dreamed of and more. There is no good and there is no bad; there is just only and always thought. As the world grows and benefits because of me, I will learn and benefit because of it! I hope that you will be able to get past these words of good and bad and elevate your mind to see the truth. Don't judge; let us love.

CHAPTER 9
WHAT DO I DO?

Luke 6:41

Why do you look at the speck of sawdust in your brother's eye and pay no attention to the plank in your own eye?

Once in the physical and once in the astrophysical (the plain of thought), you can't escape you. Your conscience is your guide. You must only do that which you agree with. What you don't agree with returns to you as an enemy! Thoughts are things. Do what YOU believe to be just, but be careful that your intent serves all. In this way, you give life to thought and flesh to words. If not, you create a destructive force that will sooner or later dissipate but not until damage is done. It's not one way you give life to words and the other way you don't. All thoughts are things! Beneficial thoughts will build while detrimental thoughts will destroy. "That you do unto the least of my brothers, you do unto me." The me in this instance Jesus speaks of is the self. God is alive in each of us. We are one, so when he speaks, it is from a personal standpoint. He comes from this standpoint to help you to acknowledge your power but to also to get you to notice the pain you bring forth, inflict and cause with just a mere thought.

We should bless with our words, but we can also bestow blessings on others, which results in blessing ourselves. Again, the least you do unto my brothers, you do unto me/yourself. So to make it clear and to bring it all the way full circle, if the least you do unto your brother you do unto me (yourself), it stands to reason that the most you do unto you brother, you do unto me/yourself as well. We must understand first what a blessing is to understand how we should set ourselves on the course to receive them. Life isn't about money and getting what you want; it's about working hard and learning lessons. As thoughts are things, the universe will make you right. The reality you say is the reality you live, because the words you say are backed by thought. The thoughts that you have must manifest themselves, because that is how the universe expands.

The power can only work through each of us. So willing or not, saint or sinner, Christian or Catholic, Hindu or of Jew, faith you will be used! I choose, in command of the free will placed inside of me, to say that I am blessed. I have trained my thoughts to think only blessings and only truth. When my thoughts stray, they are captured and subdued, and they are made to OBEY. For they are MY THOUGHTS, ARE THEY NOT? Think of this: You have children, a wife, a friend, a partner or a pet or employee or anything in your life that chooses not to obey, not to listen and not to work towards the common end we have, which should be our success. Think of that for a second. Day in and day out, you live with SOMETHING that is choosing not to help you. But not only is this SOMETHING not helping, it is destroying that which you have. It tears up the carpet and drapes, constantly empties out the accounts, is late and stirs up trouble, won't listen and is unruly. Any of these things they are, but they aren't these things sometimes; they are these things day in and day out, 24 hours in the day, 7 days a week, 30 days a month and 365 days a year. I don't know about you, but I would take some action to correct the behavior or to just rid myself of this SOMETHING. In the physical, we would take action, but in the MENTAL, why do we do nothing? Each of these things I named in the physical that offer and do harm resemble also a thought we have. We would get rid of the thing in our lives causing trouble, but how come we don't get rid of the thoughts that are doing the same damage and destruction in our lives if not ten times worse than the objects?

You will be judged for your actions and your deeds as well. This is simply seen and occurring every day of our lives. The thoughts that you have make up the thoughts that follow. You can walk around saying you are living all you want, but if there is not love in your life, you lie. The fruit you plant will appear as the fruit in your life. Thoughts are things, and this is our power to make the thought into word and the word into flesh! But we are not a people who like to self-analyze; we are a people who like to judge. Instead of studying and paying the proper attention to detail I hold to in my beliefs making sure that they are sound, I would rather judge another saying that their beliefs, since they be different from mine, are wrong. Instead of letting another pursue their thought process, we attempt to make them conform, to assimilate to our way of thinking.

Thinking has benefit when done in a group but if not constantly controlled by the individual, the group becomes a mob with no real open mind or free will at all. When that happens, we are no better, no worse and no different than an animal. Animals are the creatures made to blindly follow, not us. We were created to expand on what we see, to create new and exciting things out of the old. We were created TO AID NATURE! Nature unaided fails!

Look at New Orleans where Katrina hit, where nothing has been done and the streets and sidewalks are overturned. Look at how the vegetation now grows. In some places it resembles a third-world country, but give nature time to continue without being subdued and it will soon look like a jungle. There is no good and bad in the universe or in nature; all is known to grow, to evolve and to achieve. But, we don't put our efforts out; we turn our efforts and our thoughts in and focus them on ourselves. We try to force our beliefs and our way of thinking on another and we criticize and ridicule. We do all we can to make others be like us. When in truth, the only reason you say your way is the right way is because someone told you it was. What if they were wrong? If they were wrong but we still hold fast to old truths taught, we foolishly push an illegitimate agenda.

The only time that conflict occurs or when change is needed is when improvement is needed. You never have found yourself arguing for nothing. Conflict is nature's way of arguing. Conflict is nature's way of purging untrue and unproductive ways. This is where all war and all conflict derive from. This is why we should let men, women and especially children think freely for the betterment. Our attempt to force others into our truths is why the truth has been so distorted. The truth has turned into an agenda. The universe's agenda is the only agenda that matters. The universe's agenda is the only one that will be carried out. With this being the absolute truth, our thoughts should be geared towards us living the best and most blessed existence possible. The only way to do this is by giving that which you desire. If you give of yourself, you will receive that which you give. There is no hard work in that. The only thing that could possibly resemble work would be the study needed to understand your thoughts and how they work and can best be used to serve the whole, which at the end of the day, IS SERVING YOURSELF!

So what do I do? My answer to this is simple: I serve myself. I serve myself by my undying devotion to the thought process of serving others and being a blessing with my thoughts. I bless others with my thoughts by simply thinking and wanting good for those I see. Racism is a trick used by those who know the way to keep those who use it down. If you harbor hate for anyone, you harbor hate for yourself. A man may build up a mass fortune, but if he does not live in and honor the ways of the law, he does not live life; life lives him.

Matthew 19:24

And again I say unto you, it is easier for a camel to go through the eye of a needle, than for a rich man to enter into the kingdom of God.

The kingdom of God is thought—positive and pleasant thought. We get as we give; our duty is to make sure that we receive the most out of this life that we possibly can. It is our duty to have life and to have it more abundantly. We must have everything we desire and we should. The only way we can is to give that which we desire. That is why business owners prosper because they are constantly giving service. It doesn't matter if they work or not; everything done is done in their name. So the benefits of the thoughts bestowed is theirs. Not theirs alone, but it is theirs. They are the ones who through thought, opened up the doors and avenues for everything worth anything being done to be done. Our money is a representation of us. How you think is how you will spend your money and your time, and it is where you focus your efforts.

Look into your life; it is easy to see if you live for the whole or not. If you hold on to your money as not to let others get it, that is indeed a way to keep what you have, but how do you get more? Right now take out a dollar bill and hold it tightly in your hand so that it can't be pulled out. Pull at the dollar and it won't come out. Now, take another dollar and try to put it in the same fist. You can't; it is impossible. Now, open your hand; with an open hand you can lose but you can also receive. With an open mind, it is impossible not to receive. Your life will follow your thoughts. If you think this way, you can only be blessed this way.

I am not here to judge you; only you are here to judge you. If I am a second judge, I am only judging myself, which in turn would change the way I think into being judgmental. This would cause my life to go in a totally different direction than the one it is going in now.

Change your way by simply doing what I suggest. Take the time out to train your thoughts and to subdue your passions. You must bring your thoughts under control to truly live. You must get your thoughts to act accordingly, because they are YOUR THOUGHTS. Your thoughts represent the God in you. If not trained, they will be a total and utter disgrace.

Poem: *Looking Up*

Do I pray, do I stare or do I just contemplate your splendor? How you separated the waters to create heaven and earth, or how with mathematical precision everything moves? Never off, never out of sequence. He may not come when you need him, but he's always on time. I look up in wonder and awe, always because your shockingly amazing, never to disappoint! From the rainbow that reminds us of your covenant with the earth never to destroy it again to every desire put in the hearts of man to be extracted! Looking up, I bow my head in honor and respect to my leader, my king, my Lord, my law! I journey with you unflinchingly; the more faith I will have when our road is darkest. I will lean looking up and put my trust in you.

Chapter 10
Heaven and Hell

Matthew 12:35-36

A good man brings good things out of the good stored up in him, and an evil man brings evil things out of the evil stored up in him. But I tell you that everyone will have to give account on the Day of Judgment for every empty word they have.

My thoughts that I currently have will make up each thought that I have after this. I live in and have my reward or punishment right now; according to my faith do I receive. My heaven or hell that I live resembles to the letter the thoughts that I have. In my ability to create my thoughts, I have total control over everything that I encounter. I think and the universe follows. In death, I can only travel that groove that I have dug for myself when I had control. Nothing that exists truly dies; it is only dissipated and the configuration changed. My energy will go where it will go. Energy will be used how it will be used. My concern isn't here. My heaven or hell is in the thoughts I choose to ponder and reflect upon during my existence.

How will you use your time here? Will you create more of heaven or more of hell? We are to help in expansion; we are to affect and to inspire change. My thoughts make up each day that I encounter. I live in and am having my reward or punishment now. I think and the universe follows. In death, I can only travel that groove that I dug for myself when I had control. My energy will go where it will go. Energy will be used how it will be used. My concern isn't here. My heaven or hell is in the thoughts I choose to ponder and reflect upon. How will you use your time here? Will you create more of heaven or more of hell? If heaven is our positive thought process (only the process can be heaven), hell is our negative way of thinking but it is continuous. If you only had a single positive or negative thought, it wouldn't be heaven or hell; it would be a brief experience of each.

Most know all too well the hell that can be built with a mind and negative thoughts. We know all too well this existence because that is the one that most CHOOSE to live in and be a part of. Many of us are prisoners of our own thoughts. We have lost the control of our thoughts and we can no longer even attempt to deal with them. We cling to devices and anything else mechanical or otherwise that would serve to offer escape.

Proverbs 31:6

Let beer be for those who are perishing, wine for those who are in anguish! Let them drink and forget their poverty and remember their misery no more.

The more we seek to escape our thoughts, the more we become trapped by them. Most often the hell you seek to escape is the hell you draw ever closer to in thought. When we seek to run from a situation instead of dealing with it, we let thoughts of this thing grow like weeds in our minds. So as you physically seek to escape your troubles, you draw them nearer because you are continuously thinking of the situation. You should draw out and design in great detail the hell that you now occupy. I say do this because in your mind you are doing the same, so why not draw it out?

What isn't understood is that there is an artist in your mind, and his skill set surpasses Rembrandt and even Picasso himself in the painting of the masterpiece that you see in your mind. You hold that vision so steadily and so clearly in mind that the force can't help but to get down every last detail. Your thoughts reproduce and reproduce and reproduce until finally the end result is a masterpiece, the very one you held in your mind. It is a direct reflection of the picture you had in your head. The life you live is only made possible through the thoughts that you daily have and entertain. If you live in hell right now because of these very reasons I state, be ye not afraid because heaven and all you seek for your happiness is just a thought away. Just think, the same amount of hell that we endure that you go through right now, could be matched by the same amount of heaven that lies in our thoughts. If trained to, you could now begin to think of nothing but heaven. Heaven and hell are merely states of mind.

Over time, as you train yourself to close your eyes and see hell, also train yourself to close your eyes and see heaven. See yourself as you would see yourself if you were perfect. You are perfection, in every sense of the word. If you have trained yourself to believe a lie that says you are dumb, stupid and unworthy, it should be just as easy for you to train yourself to believe the truth. By thinking your heaven into existence, it will come.

What is your vision of the perfect you? Don't let the word perfection scare you. It is all about paying attention to detail. Nobody has ever bought a dirty car. It must be detailed and clean to attract our attention. The universe is the same way; attract it by the use of your imagination. Catch the universe's eye with this vision you have to elevate the whole. Dream so big that you even impress yourself. Up until now, you have been dreaming so low that you are sick. If you are ever in doubt as to what to think, remember how you used to see your life and think the total opposite. The second that you are able to lift yourself out of hell, YOU BETTER STOP, TURN AROUND AND THROW DOWN A LADDER TO THE NEXT ONE CLIMBING, BECAUSE DAMMIT, WE NEED HELP!

Now we come to the part of the conversation dealing with the heaven or the hell that we can create for another. In the blessing or in the cursing of others with your thought, you do this. You can build another up or you can tear them down. You will be rewarded for one and judged for the other.

James 1:26-27

Those who consider themselves religious and yet do not keep a tight rein on their tongues deceive themselves, and their religion is worthless. Religion that God our Father accepts as pure and faultless is this: to look after orphans and widows in their distress and to keep oneself from being polluted by the world.

In cursing or being a blessing to others, you are able to build up your heaven or hell in your mind brick by brick. Remember that each thought breeds another thought that breeds another thought until at last you get what you come in contact with. No thought is unimportant. All thoughts are like starfish in that each thought can reproduce another thought without any help from an outside source. Our thoughts reproduce like rabbits. That is why it's said that an idle mind is the devil's workshop.

There are hundreds of things produced in a workshop in a single day. Now figure what the power of negative thought can do over a lifetime. It's enough to make you never want to have another negative thought again. If we didn't have any more negative thoughts, what kind of things could we think about? We could think things like, I love my children in spite of their faults because they are mine and I'm far from perfect. We could think thoughts like, I promise to help the next 7 people I see, and every week I promise to help others a little one more. We could think thoughts like, I'm going to send out happy thoughts every time I see someone smile. All these thoughts will inspire another thought until they overrun your mind like roaches left to breed in a house full of food. Now clearly, if this is the case, the way that you think and operate now is a result of the babies your initial thoughts had back when you first had that initial thought.

Vow to never curse another again. Reconcile that in yourself is a huge industrial factory and the only machines that you make are good thought machines. Each machine is capable of producing mass amounts of positivity all on its own. Now, imagine that you are setting off on a journey to make others happy and feel loved. Start up your own personal "good thoughts for people" club. Let your slogan be: I'M NOT ONLY THE PRESIDENT OF THE COMPANY, BUT I'M ALSO A MEMBER!

Poem: *When I'm Lonely*

I take time to think about how that could never be! How I'm a part of creation and everything that exists has a piece of me in it. Me being lonely with this in mind is absurd! How could I be ignorant enough to deny my birthright, the fact that I'm eternally connected to the vine! That when everything on earth was made, it was made with me in mind! How would the sun, moon grass, clouds and stars make me feel? That was definitely contemplated before the final mold of everything was cast! My personality permeates the cosmos! When I feel alienated, I'm honest with myself in that I alone am at the base of that feeling of loneliness, of singular, of separate! For who could convince me my father has turned away other than myself? If a stranger tried the same he would be laughed out of existence! It is only myself that could convince me that I'm lonely! Rather, I will convince myself that I am an invaluable piece to this machine called humanity, called together, called life. Lonely, impossible unless I choose to be!

CHAPTER 11
DO I CONVINCE YOU OR DO YOU NEED PROOF?

Ephesians 1:19

And what is the exceeding greatness of his power to us who believe, according to the working of his mighty power.

What words can I express to you to convince you that what I say is the truth? Should I create beautiful poetry or sonnets? No, that has been done already. Should I make songs that express the truth in its words? No, that has been done also. Should I write a single book full of many different authors, each inspired by the truth and label it the Bible? No, that has been done as well, plus it won't be believed. The truth is this: There are no words that can be said to make you believe. Your thoughts will lean as they do, either towards this way or away from this way. It is really up to you; your free WILL must be exercised. Have your mind, ears and eyes been closed so long to the point that they can no longer see and hear? Are they no longer able to receive or to decipher the word of truth? Has your mind been so closed that it will even push away from what it yearns for and needs to grow?

The truth is you don't need to be convinced; you now read, have and possess truth again because thoughts are things and you pulled it to yourself. Somewhere, at some point inside, you said to yourself, "Self, I want to know." And poof, just like magic, here I AM. Not me, but me—your thought in the form of what you now hold. Is it that hard to believe that you are so loved by the universe that it would help you to understand? It diligently seeks to help you do anything else. It allows you to summon anything from knowledge to poverty. People believe in God or a higher power. Is it that difficult to contemplate that he loved us so much that he gave us the ability to control our surroundings with thought? If you believe in him/in it—the power to be so powerful—this shouldn't impress you/us/me for a second. If we are embodied with the all-powerful essence of the creator, shouldn't we look for and even come to expect his favor? We should if we have studied. Even if we haven't, you feel the favor deep in your bones. You feel the favor because it is your birthright. You live the ability to create thoughts into things.

Our mind is made up of positive energy. Electrons are of negative pulse but they also contain tiny, microscopic bits of metal. The positive vibration of our minds is scientifically proven to be able to manipulate these particles. We manipulate these pieces of everything created with our thought. First, we think; once a thought is had, the thought does an amazing thing. It induces a chain reaction to occur. Electrons move with protons and neutrons to form atoms. Atoms, as we all know, form matter. Everything you see in front of you with your eyes is comprised of matter. This is the truth, so much so that you can follow everything seen by your eyes in this world; you can follow it back to a thought originated by a single person or a group of individuals. Start at your home and follow each thing that you see back to the thought that it originated from. You will clearly be able to now understand the power that lies within you. You can believe this to be a lie, you can use every story contrary to this to ATTEMPT to disprove (but you won't; the truth this is, so it be absolute), or you could begin to right now learn you. You could right now acknowledge that you are going to be judged for your deeds and thoughts.

If I were a child in school and talked in class, you would tell me to adjust my behavior and to control it. If truly we are to be judged for action and deed, and if I can control my behavior, it would stand to reason that I can control the thought that precipitated it. Since I can control my thought, I can control what I receive in life. I bring to myself that which I think. If my thoughts are controlled, I will regulate my outcome in life with ease.

Since we have all originated from the vine, I embody my God, myself and my fellow man. Let your spirit be free to feed; it is starving for the truth. Either you will or you won't; I love you EITHER WAY because YOU ARE ME, WE ARE WE and HE BE US! Will you come in out of the rain? If you won't accept, will you at least entertain that which you hear? Your free WILL is the only way you can receive; there is no force and no motivation. If I force you, you will turn from this way once you are out of my sight. If I use my words to motivate you, once the sound of my voice wears off, you will leave to seek the next source of motivation. No—either you do or you don't; either you will or you won't. In the meantime, be honest with yourself in that you truly do think things into existence. If you only thought like God thinks, which is always giving, you would be as the universe is: always receiving. There is no way you would experience lack of any kind

Use your power so that you can see that strength which you possess. After testing and evaluating what you need to test and to evaluate, come back and grab this book to learn all that you need to know to use your thought power for your benefit. Why fight against what you could possibly use for your help? Never should you blindly accept anything because another says you should, but at least give your mind a chance to study and to understand what it is attempting to digest before you come up with 101 reasons not to believe and to question without thought what you have heard. If you would question this truth in that manner, in what way did you deal with the man who first brought this news? Did you question the preacher, your mother or the teacher? I'm sure you didn't question him or them in this way because if you did, this book would hold no relevance to your life. It would hold no relevance because you already know how to think, and you use the power now because you already understand everything I am attempting through the power to let you see through me.

John14:11

Believe me when I say that I am in the Father and the Father is in me; or at least believe on the evidence of the works themselves.

You will think as you will, because you have no other choice; your WILL is your way. If you don't like the way that you think, use your WILL to change that way. You have all abilities; to begin to use them, all you need to do is to begin to use them. Give yourself a chance to understand, have faith and believe. Believe in that thing that you have been taught is helpless: yourself! Do I need to convince you? Or will you just believe?

Poem: *Only Love on My Lips and Praise in My Heart*

There is only love on my lips and praise in my heart, so I will fear no evil. His rod and staff of love and praise protect my soul. Let each be a constant reminder to me so that I never break our bond or our connection—the connection that joins us on a cosmic level, the connection that keeps only love on my lips and praise in my heart. It is on my knees I praise and with my mind's mouth I express and relay vibes and thoughts of pure love so I may play my part. My part in sharing the peace you've guaranteed me from birth, my right. The peace that keeps only love on my lips and praise in my heart! The peace you freely give to all those who accept YOU! With the endless combinations of thought that this mind granted to me can accomplish in making words flesh, it is my duty to only keep love on my lips and praise in my heart..

Chapter 12
Must We Earn Our Birthright?

1 John 4:16-17

And so we know and rely on the love God has for us. God is love. Whoever lives in love lives in God, and God in them. This is how love is made complete among us so that we will have confidence on the Day of Judgment. In this world we are like Jesus.

Your ability to think was provided by the creator. Every word spoken or action taken is precipitated by thought. I think therefore I AM. God is the great I AM, and we are made divinely in his image, less one degree. The more you believe, the more you can do, and this idea will be expanded upon in the chapter on apparatuses. Whether you are atheist, Christian, Buddhist, Jewish or Mormon, whichever you are, you think, and that's what makes you worthy. You did nothing to possess this power. You can improve upon it and you can add to it, but you did nothing so great as to possess, have, obtain or bestow the power of thought.

We bestow this power through our part played in childbirth: creation. Your birthright is your divine ability to think; what you use it for is up to you. Religion and philosophy are just a means to keep your thoughts straight, lofty and expanding. These things were created to expand the mind, but over the years of the knowledge being passed, they resemble more a cage than a means of escape. However, no one is on the outside of faith. As a man thinketh, so shall he be.

The person with 50 years of faith or a babe with just a mustard seed of faith both have enough. Study to learn your power, not to receive it. You go to church to keep your thoughts straight, not to wash your sins away and not to be forgiven. You can only forgive yourself for your past deeds, and if you do forgive yourself, you will be forgiven and born to a new way of thinking. You forgive yourself and it's evident because you no longer think, speak and act as you once did. You no longer go to the same places or even have the same friends because you have changed your mind. "Change your mind"—the phrase seems so innocent but no statement could be more powerful. If you change your mind, you change the way you think, and if you change the way you think, you change your life.

1 Corinthians 13:11

> *When I was a child, I talked like a child, I thought like a child, I reasoned like a child. When I became a man, I put the ways of childhood behind me.*

Our birthright, this divine ability, is and goes disregarded. Like children, we only go to the source FOR wants, dreams desires and wishes. But if we commune for communion's sake, we can receive instruction, direction and guidance. If we would allow ourselves to BE STILL, we could then be led to loftier thoughts by the thoughts we let grow, manifest and mature. Unearthly treasures as well as earthly ones are a mere thought away. You did nothing to earn this right but be born. For God so loved the world that he gave us the ability to think. Without thought, we would have no need for salvation. Without thought, being saved from our sins would be meaningless, like a dog going to church. It is only because of our birthright that we can even appreciate the power we serve. The power meets us at our level; it loves all of its children and wants the ones who will return to come home.

1 Corinthians 9:19-22

Though I am free and belong to no one, I have made myself a slave to everyone, to win as many as possible. To the Jews I became like a Jew, to win the Jews. To those under the law I became like one under the law (though I myself am not under the law), so as to win those under the law. To those not having the law I became like one not having the law (though I am not free from God's law but am under Christ's law), so as to win those not having the law.

To the weak I became weak, to win the weak. I have become all things to all people so that by all possible means I might save some.

The power is everything we need. It is our birthright; we all have the ability to think. But with this birthright, whom do you serve? As it is you right from birth, your free will to "DO WHAT THOUGH WILT," do you put your efforts towards the whole or towards yourself? Our thought is our right, yes, but it was bestowed not earned. Our mission, whether accepted or not, is to further the kingdom. Let us not take our existence for granted; we are the chosen ones because we are here on this planet with an ability that matches that of the creator. What shall we create? Shall we meet weekly and keep this blessing, our birthright, secret? Or will we take to the streets and profess to all who will listen? You are not forced to play your part, but your part is being played whether you accept your role or not. The acceptance of your role is only to make your journey easier while you are on it. To accept your role is to begin to attempt to understand thought. "I think therefore I AM." I AM also because I think. This cannot be disproven; the words say it all. You could not say I AM if you were not. This is not said and done in an attempt to confuse you. The fact that you are is your birthright, and there is power in every birthright; that's why it is bestowed on those worthy of it.

1 Chronicles 5:2

Though Judah was the strongest of his brothers and a ruler came from him, the rights of the firstborn belonged to Joseph.

We are here blessed with a birthright that allows us to order our steps. With the knowledge contained in these pages, you can be a light unto your own path. In times of despair, you do not have to seek any other than yourself. You embody all that has been manifested since the beginning of time. Shared with and inside of you are all the mysteries of the cosmos—all of the glorious combinations of thought to be utilized and had. My thought is not me conjuring up anything. My thought making the word into flesh in my existence for me to enjoy is as natural as childbirth. I AM but one degree removed from the master. He is the father and I am the son.

We all possess the spirit that navigates the cosmos. If I don't possess this spirit, then how am I able to think? For thinking is the ultimate and only God quality that you can think of. Because every amazing thing that you can think of to say that God or anyone does, for that matter, is inspired, fueled and backed by thought!

Claiming our birthright is us finally acknowledging our creator in the way in which he was always meant to be honored. If we continue living like sheep, moving blindly, we will never reach our full potential. It is up to us to learn and to explore our divinity. If we do not, we are no different than cattle. And cattle are no different than the slave who buried his coin. You are WRONG for not expanding on what you have been given, and you will be dealt with in the end.

Luke 12:47

The servant who knows the master's will and does not get ready or does not do what the master wants will be beaten with many blows.

If you are not receiving and utilizing your birthright, the blows that befall you are the blows of thought—your illegitimate, misguided thoughts. You must take back your power at all cost. You must wrestle it away, fight to get it free and kill the one who keeps it from you if necessary. The one you must do battle with, the one you must kill to win back your birthright, is yourself, because you, your mind, your thoughts, these things you hold to be true with no study to back it are the things that are separating you from understanding your lineage and the divinity you were blessed enough to inherent at birth. My Lord (Thought) is my shepherd, I shall not want. I shall not want because I have the ability to make words flesh. I have the ability through thought to do more than just merely exist. I possess great power that can be used to exact change. I possess great power and I did nothing to earn it, because it is MY BIRTHRIGHT!

Poem: *I Truly AM*

Every name you can think of to describe perfect, for in his image I am made! As we all are, powerful and perfect in every regard. Able to understand and know! I truly am as we all are, /only/as blessed, special, and stupendous as I give myself credit for being. That's why I am, everything, under the sun and more, for I truly am my father's son! But the power lies in the fact that I know that I TRULY AM!

Chapter 13
There Is Nothing New under the Sun

Psalm 23:1-6

The LORD is my shepherd, I lack nothing. He makes me lie down in green pastures, he leads me beside quiet waters, he refreshes my soul. He guides me along the right paths for his name's sake.

Even though I walk through the darkest valley, I will fear no evil, for you are with me; your rod and your staff, they comfort me. You prepare a table before me in the presence of my enemies. You anoint my head with oil; my cup overflows. Surely your goodness and love will follow me all the days of my life, and I will dwell in the house of the LORD forever.

We have been here before; I say this with all certainty. It is a proven scientific fact that no matter is destroyed. A selected form may die and dissipate, but its energy, its life force is re-injected back into the whole. Its energy and force may be given to another configuration of energy and be forced to go and propitiate evolution. It is this way in everything; if it was not, life as we know it would cease to exist. Any combination of numbers will eventually run out, but numbers themselves are infinite. The truth of this can be seen in the change of area codes or three-digit codes eventually turning to four digits due to the inevitable exhaustion of sequences. So life itself, life as we know it, is always evolving and always changing in an effort to never end. With this being said, everything that you are comprised of everything that makes you up is not new; it is just energy and force reconfigured into a new combination for the time being. The structure created is new, but the materials used to create it have been around since the beginning of time itself.

If we have been here since the beginning of time and no matter is destroyed but just reconfigured, aren't we connected because we are part of the vine? If I was comprised from the whole and when I die I/you we will return back to it, it would stand to reason that during my time on earth, I am still connected to it because it is impossible to break the connection. And if it be the whole that it is filled with all knowledge and has been observant of all things since the beginning of time, it would stand to reason that I could access this knowledge when needed. It can never be overlooked that all is done to expand and to help with the evolution of existence. No task or thing needed to help with the accomplishment of this task is too great. The Wright brothers only had an idea of flying, Bill Gates only had an idea of the computer and we only have the ideas that we have. These ideas are made to come true because each helps in some way to expand creation!

We live by chance, when we could just as easily live by fact. I say by chance because for most, success is hit or miss. If, before speaking, we accessed the great knowledge that has been accumulated for eons, we would never lose. We can touch it and partake of its bounty the same as we do the library. We can mentally access this storehouse of knowledge according to our faith. As to your faith, what you need to know will be revealed. Believe me when I say this power you have exists. It more than just exists; it has been used by those who prosper since the beginning of time. Some people are fully aware of what power they use in gaining success and they hide the answers to keep away the competition. There are others like myself who now and always have spoken freely about the power, telling all that I see. But most whom I tell, regard what I say. They disregard what I say as rhetoric, mumbo-jumbo or something they are too young, too old or just aren't ready for. Preachers talk according to their degree of understanding, but not all truly understand. Being able to eloquently recite that which you have studied does not make you know the truth, much less understand it. It does however make you an excellent orator. I want answers, not just words that sound like they are answer-filled. These words that sound answer-filled insight me to want to know, to want to believe, to want to get to the truth, but at the end of the day, after they have been deflated (these words) and the music dies down, I am left alone sitting with the same questions I sought answers to from the start.

These leaders of industry figured out the answers, which can be summed up in one word: FAITH. Everyone will use it, educated or not. But you must agree with me on this: If you find yourself in a house designed by Bill Gates, a house totally of the future, you must agree that a person who has no knowledge of technology wouldn't get the same enjoyment out of the home that a computer technician would. That is the same as with you and your mind. If you knew what you were capable of, you would do more. We have been here since the beginning of time. Knowing that you are made up of what it takes to make up life itself should give us each a different energy towards life.

I'm saying here and now that you are created from the same substance that makes up everything, and that you can access this power if you would just train yourself as to how. I say that all things that you can conceive you can achieve. I say that the universe will give you the tools you need to create, build, and accomplish anything that you can fathom. Think of the creator as having a huge job watching over us. He/IT/the power doesn't have the time to keep an eye on each in the physical sense of watching over us, but it/he watches out for us and sends the supplies that we require is because we are hardwired to it/him. Our thoughts once had are directly connected to the source. As soon as we think it and put desire into the thought, we begin to attract it. Or better put, it is immediately released in our direction. Once released, your belief in its arrival will dictate the timeline in which you receive it. If you think in terms of it not happening, it never will. If you believe it will come right on time, then you understand. We have been here since the beginning of time and we can access this power at any time.

1 Corinthians 2:4-5

My message and my preaching were not with wise and persuasive words, but with a demonstration of the Spirit's power, so that your faith might not rest on human wisdom, but on God's power.

YYou can be anything you want with this power. You can create endless things. It doesn't matter if you couldn't go to a school that you couldn't afford. YOU ARE BRILLIANT! Why would you think any less of yourself? I BEG YOU, get up. Learn this power and become one with the understanding of it because you are already its own. It is the WILL of the universe that you receive and be equipped with all the knowledge and everything you need to impact creation and evolution in the greatest way. Rise in your view of yourself! Rise in your perception of the power so that you may rise in your personal utilization of it. Think of something that you can't possibly now attain. If you contemplate on that thought long enough, you will begin to think up ways to get it until it is yours. That is the power being accessed, except you had no knowledge of it. You may have not even received because some of the avenues presented you didn't take. Or you attempted to take it from another person instead of creating it with your own power. In all cases, you couldn't get or keep it. The only way to possess and retain a thing is to create it yourself. And the only way to create or to bring a blueprint to fruition is to be specific and to pay attention to detail. You must access all your stores of knowledge regarding this subject and be meticulous in your efforts. That is all that is needed to rebuild yourself in the power and to access all its storehouses of information. EVERYTHING STARTS WITH A THOUGHT!

Poem: *No Hesitation*

One cannot hesitate; you must seize the day. Moments are fleeting, gone in the blink of an eye, never to be regained, only to be reminisced or lamented upon. You must take what is yours, but you can only have that. Another's in your hands will have a short lifespan. Not quickly but without hesitation, the difference is preciseness in movement. For a move to be made without hesitation, you must be mentally on your toes at all times. Clear and precise thinking, without pause. No hesitation!

CHAPTER 14
THE UNIVERSE MAKES YOU RIGHT!

Jeremiah 5:31

The prophets prophesy lies, the priests rule by their own authority, and my people love it this way. But what will you do in the end?

Through thought, the universe makes you right. If you believe yourself to be a failure, you will be. Watch what you wish for; you just might get it. Know what you are contemplating/thinking of, because good or bad, it's on its way. The universe and our divine thought process work hand in hand to further creation. The master works through us to aid nature and humanity. We have been chosen and given a great power, a power that makes us what we think. Everything we do expands creation in some way. For us to be denied thought is for the universe to stop growing. We know that to be impossible and unnatural. Nothing in nature is neutral. All in nature is either living or dying. The second we are born, we know someday we will die. This is the inevitable cycle of life. The most important decision we have been charged with making is the way in which you WILL choose to use your thought power in between these two events: life and death. Who are you, my brother and sister? Who do you say that you are? Who do you think you are?

Understand that this thought that you have of yourself, this way that you think of you, this way that you see and think of yourself backed by the belief you have of it being true, makes up exactly what you see in the mirror. If you are pleased at the sight you behold in your mind of yourself, then fine. But if the true thought of you when you close your eyes isn't what you want to see, all you need to do to change this thought is to change the thoughts that have led you to think this way.

When I was young, I was told that the only man who knows anything is the man who knows he knows nothing. I wrestled with that until I understood it to mean this: What you may know is always changing, so what is needed to keep up is an open mind, which is a mind that has the ability to inherently and instinctively think freely outside of the box and problem solve. In everything you do and even attempt, keep an open mind. With this open mind, you now see yourself, not as you in your thoughts see yourself, but you see yourself as that person who you want to become. It is the person who if you did everything correctly, you would be. Think of him or her down to the very last detail you could describe. This you imagine is being created and any missed detail would mean an inferior product. Mentally iron out all of your rough edges and all of the things that you wish you didn't do. See this new you as in control of every part of you where you want to be. See even your dress; see it all. See it so clearly that this vision of the new you is now what you see in your mind when you picture yourself. Before long, you will resemble this thought. You will also notice that the OLD YOU will fade away. What you see in your mind is backed by your will. As it says in the Bible, THY WILL BE DONE!

Let's consider for a BRIEF moment the old you and what it took for you to arrive there. The old you is old, dead and gone. The only you that is present now is what you saw when you used a new set of eyes. The old you did not just happen to appear. He/she was created by the same process. The universe granted you every thought you had about you until what you saw before you was the final product. The universe/God does not stop you from experiencing all you can in this world. However, the power takes for granted that you, as a child of divinity, truly use your power of thought. The power takes for granted that you use your WILL to produce. To produce only those things that would serve to help you and seek to further your life, not to hurt you and seek to destroy it. But the fact remains, we are given the free WILL to think and to choose for yourself that which you will. You are not forced to pick one path over another.

All paths of thought lead to the expansion of the universe. A particular line of thought will serve to bring about a better day-to-day existence for yourself. A different way of thought will serve to use the power of the universe to construct heaven for yourself. The old you that you saw was what he was because you thought him up to be that way. Many of us don't want that kind of power, as it may seem frightening from the start. With scientific thought, all that isn't understood will reveal itself.

This power that we have to always be right takes skill and understanding to wield. We are powerful, but we are also responsible. We are responsible to ourselves to think with caution and to exercise great restraint. Your thoughts create you, so if you have thoughts of help, service and what's best for the whole, you will be able to maintain the vision you saw in your mind of the new you. But if you have thoughts contrary to these, thoughts similar to those that created the old you, then you will go back to being that old you. You will dig up that dead body and climb right back inside. We think up the suit of skin that we are wrapped in.

Please understand that if you perceive yourself to be God or the devil, it is you who thought you up. You use your thoughts to guide the universe's power in the lines that it should travel to bring your provisions. If you take a lofty road of thought, you will resemble that. It will be evident in all you do. If you choose to take the low road, you will resemble that. Your thoughts and deeds will resemble plots and schemes. Your thought will produce the physical equivalent unto its kind. You can never trick the universe into making you into something you are not. If you ever want to know what another thinks, listen to their words while observing their lives. You will be made aware.

The universe is our Father, and the universe gives us all we ask for. The power will sustain us and be with us whenever we need it. It has been all of our lives; it is the reason we can say I AM. This power so apparent and able is overlooked. Not unused, just overlooked. It could never go unused because we are always thinking. I say that it goes overlooked because we are not always thinking properly.

We are all different; no two snowflakes are alike. We will never think the same on all issues. I still say that we think improperly however because we think of things that will hurt instead of help us. We think low thoughts of personal gain, not gain for all. Think of the universal supply like a stream of water through a garden hose. If you think in terms of only that which can benefit you, you are squeezing the hose as the water comes out so the supply is not as great. But when you think in terms of the whole and what could best help all, the stream flows with the force and the pressure of a fire hose hooked to a fire hydrant. All power is in thought but the amount of power received is governed by its intended use. Leaders of industry are looked at negatively, but they are truly the few who are using their thought power to benefit all, not just a few. You think in terms of their money, but in truth, every customer had their life enhanced by some way by the idea shared by this individual. And if that isn't focusing on the whole of humanity, I don't know for the life of me what else is.

You see yourself as broken and poor, and you are right! You see yourself as stupid and ghetto; you are right. You see yourself as a servant and a worker; you are right. Now my question to you is this: Are these the only ways that we can see ourselves? It's not about color, because every race has their indigent. The indigent think indulgently. The universe expresses through you all that you envision. It grants you that which you require. If this is true, which it is, why do you ask for strength to maintain instead of the strength it takes to triumph? Why do you ask to be made a supervisor, when you are suited better to be boss? Why do we ask for hamburger instead of steak? Why do we ask for a house instead of a mansion? A man can only rise as high as his highest thought.

Please, my brothers and sisters, right now look around and see what the inside of your mind looks like. Thoughts are things, and your highest thought is always around you. Now, look at a millionaire's house; understand that you are seeing his highest thought. The things that surround him, all that he encounters, all that we encounter in a day are but a mere reflection of our highest thought.

What's your highest thought? Before you answer that, stop and raise it by 10. Then in time, by ten again until you die. I say raise it by ten in this way because your highest thought has you living how you are living now. If you are satisfied, then by all means disregard this book. But if for a second all that you are isn't all that you want to be, change that which you think you know.

1 Corinthians 8:2

And if any man think that he knows anything, he knows nothing yet as he ought to know.

Poem: *Electrons*

Keep my mind free, loved ones please pray for me
That I am able to see what's as elusive as a breeze
It's ok my mind is a positive and able to attract
That's why I focus on no lack
I just give more and get that back
Now that's a scientific fact as 1+1 is 2
That what you do to others will surely be done unto you.
To state that much more plain we will be judged for actions and deeds.
It is not the sin that befalls the son, it's truly what he sees.

Because as we think so as we are again in the scientific realm.
Negative captain or positive captain it is you who's at the helm
What you think you see please believe me
That life is lived in the spiritual place
That look of wonder was had in mind before it ever reached your face
Electrons make atoms and molecules are next
Which forms the mass of the things you amass with all the wasted checks.
But think of this if but for a blink or the time it takes a grin to fade
What we could do if constructive and true all our thoughts were made!

CHAPTER 15
SCIENTIFIC THOUGHT

Ecclesiastes 9:4

Anyone who is among the living has hope—even a live dog is better off than a dead lion!

We are blessed with amazing power! With great power comes greater responsibility. Our great power is thought. This is a super human quality, one only possessed by the gods. To be bestowed with such a great power, we must learn and grow to control it. Thought power to the untrained is like putting a gun into a child's hands. Just think what panic, danger and chaos would ensue the situation of a child with a loaded deadly weapon. This is the same situation that occurs when you have a group of grown men and women walking the earth who don't know how to think. We have panic, chaos and danger occurring. Unscientific thought brings about these ends, but scientific thought will induce the total opposite.

Scientific thought involves merely controlling one's mind. This type of thought transforms the mind into a garden and your thoughts into seeds. Positive thought produces beautiful flowers and negative thoughts produce weeds. The job of any gardener is to keep his garden weed-free. He diligently keeps tabs on all thoughts and pulls those ones that are detrimental to the beauty of his garden. You are doing the same by staying mindful of your thoughts and irradiating all those negative thoughts/weeds that would seek to choke the life out of your positive thoughts/beautiful flowers. Make no mistake, any weed/ negative thought, whether big or small, seeks to kill, steal and destroy all flowers/positive thoughts. But negativity/the devil is a lie! Darkness is only the absence of light. Darkness can hold no power over you if you have light! Light in this instance is merely an understanding of who you are and the great power you control. With the knowledge of "This little light of mine," you could never be in darkness. Your little light is your mustard seed. It is small initially, but if you plant that seed and let nature take its course, it will grow.

We know we have thought power, so the next question is this: How are we supposed to maximize our thought power? We should always think in terms of the whole or in terms of the Golden Rule. "Do unto others as you would have them to do unto you." This seems juvenile to some, but in all actuality, it is a training process in keeping your thoughts straight. If you only think in terms of the whole, or treat others as you would be treated, you're able to order your steps.

In thought, we bring all that we contemplate to our doorsteps. This is a fact. Contemplate the arrival of the last thing you received. Think back to the thought that precipitated it. If you are honest with yourself and take the time to retrace the thing back to the thought that brought it to fruition, you will see the power, majesty and overwhelming effects of thought. If you had the time, you could trace all the things in your life back to the thought that started the result you experience in motion. If honed, refined and paid attention to, you can get your thoughts to be what you would like them to be. Every thought you have sets up a tire track or groove for the rest of the thoughts that follow. This groove also insures the thoughts will resemble the thought that precipitated it. It's truly a game of follow the leader.

You can't serve two masters so in your mind, there will be a predominant thought. You have the power to change that predominate thought if it's not the thought that you desire. You know if the thoughts that you are having are desired or not by the effect they have on your life. Your thoughts are things, so you think. When these thoughts are manifested, do they help or hurt? Do they please or do they torment you? If you are experiencing the first, perfect. If you are enduring the latter, all you need is to change how you think and you will change what you experience. I'm sure the possibilities of this statement are frightening. They induce fear because we truly don't want that control. For if we are in total control, who can we blame for mistakes? Better put, if all things are perfect in the moment and everything facilitates evolution, is there even such a thing as a mistake? Or is it just an adverse circumstance produced? If that be the case, it's never the situation but how you deal with it.

Failure, defeat and loss are the biggest tools of learning, reception and maturity ever created. The more your mind expands, the more you understand. The more you understand, the more you can do. The more you can do, the more you can be used to do other things. The power can only work through us for others and through others for us.

Proverbs 11:25

A generous person will prosper, whoever refreshes others will be refreshed.

If you give and offer help to others, you carry the thought of giving and helping. The brother and sister to giving and helping is receiving and support. If you give pain and contrary thoughts, you will also receive this. This is a simple truth! The beautiful thing is the simplicity in it all. If you begin to scientifically think, that is to be aware of your thoughts as they happen and only allow those positive thoughts or thoughts of your achievement, acceleration and prosperity, what will eventually happen is this: Equate the thoughts you have to a tire track in deep snow on the freeway. The first car that made that track has no traction, the next car had a little more and the next a little more until final a tread was formed. Now on the freeway, all cars that follow have a clear path. These are your thoughts. At first, positivity may seem difficult but after each thought, it will get easier until finally the way is formed. And this precipitates a beautiful thing in nature.

The involuntary movement of your thoughts become a habit. When you train your thoughts to behave positively, after time they do so on their own. That is the snowball of faith rolling down. Once you have trained your thoughts to give, your rate of reception will be out of control. It will feel like the windows of heaven have opened up and poured out blessings upon you that after being shaken and packed, they will still overflow.

What you are seeking is seeking you; it is easier to seek negative thoughts with an untrained mind. But once trained, negative thoughts will be noticed, subdued and eradicated like mice in a home. Once the mind is trained, you will be able to control your thoughts like we do electricity. With the flip of a switch, or a flip of your WILL, you will be able to order your steps. Not even continually anymore; they will just be and stay positive because the groove will become a trench. Your thoughts will become greater and greater as they evolve in their attempt to emulate the thought that they follow. It is a lovely orchestra put to the music of thought. The score choreographs itself in perfect harmony through no further action of your own than that taken from the beginning when you received and began to follow.

You can see the importance of treating others the way that you would have them treat you. This is to get you to make that first tire track. We follow blindly, or stumble onto the path through religion or philosophy reciting rhetoric, but we never truly understand what is meant and what is being said! It is easy, a small thing to even a child, to read the word. But to decipher it and understand it correctly is the chore. I dare never say, "I know!" One thing a man knows is the fact that he truly knows nothing. This is the first step to keeping an open mind. I never would say that I have the answers, but how does the truth make you feel? If the truth moves you, it is for good reason. It is because it is time for you to move. If this message was not for you and didn't possess the power to answer your questions and to put yourself on the path you seek, you would not have it in your hands. But it is up to you to scientifically choose to think and accept it. An open mind will open you up to it possibly being a new way of thinking. But your soul, heart, thoughts and spirit will tell you if it is the right way. You must have the courage to follow. In spite of what your friends, family onlookers and anyone else may say, HOW DOES THE TRUTH MAKE YOU FEEL?

Poem: *The WORD*

In the beginning there was the WORD and IT was the WORD and the WORD was all that was needed. Progress has brought about much change. But what has remained a constant is the power of the WORD. Precipitated by thought once heard is in motion. Backed by feeling and the persistence of will. The WORD made flesh. God said let there be light and since spoken, mankind has been forever illuminated. The WORD, taken for granted, used incorrectly but your power never weans! Possessing as much impact as when spoken by him in the deep to start all seen. As it is now when uttered by the intelligent or fool alike; Adult or child-POWERFUL it is. The WORD, a church in itself.

Chapter 16

The Bible: A Living Breathing Book of Thought

2 John 1:6

And this is love: that we walk in obedience to his commands. As you have heard from the beginning, his command is that you walk in love.

Thought is what gives the Bible life, not the word. The Bible points always to the godliness in thought. The power of the word is a bi-product of thought. Money is an expression of understanding. The word is an expression of thought. The Bible always points to this. It does this by always emphasizing the power in the word. If there be so much power in the word, the true source be thought. Because no word can be uttered without first being thought. Conceive to achieve. You must first think it before it can be done. The Bible is designed to train us how to think; every scenario known to man is in the Bible. It recollects the situations that were incurred and the ways in which they were dealt with. It explains what is expected of us by the power as well as by nature. It explains to us how to think, while also showing us the power of thought. The Bible shows the benefit of having discipline but it emphasizes keeping an open mind. The Bible is a blueprint to living in a world encompassed by the powers of the cosmos. Philosophy has its own Bible. The Bible of philosophy is filled with the sayings that we hear. Bible verses and sayings alike are all to act as a trellis to help us keep our thoughts straight and upright.

Let's for a moment view our thoughts like roses. A rose possesses great beauty but it also embodies pain in the form of thorns. Many are not aware of this fact but a rose is both a weed and a flower. It is both because a weed by definition is something growing somewhere you don't want it to grow. Thoughts are a lot like roses, in that some are beautiful and others can grow like weeds. What makes a rose look so pretty is the care that it's given, but mostly it is so beautiful because of the attention to detail given to it so that it grows straight. We must be the same way with our thoughts.

Always pay close attention to each thought. We pay such close attention so that they all will win first prize at the state fair. When we see a thought going astray, we quickly rein it back it. When one thought seeks to strangle another thought, we must pull it from the soil, less it may destroy the whole bush. Our minds are so important, but we regard them not.

Isaiah 55: 8-11

"For my thoughts are not your thoughts, neither are your ways my ways," declares the LORD. "As the heavens are higher than the earth, so are my ways higher than your ways and my thoughts than your thoughts. As the rain and the snow come down from heaven, and do not return to it without watering the earth and making it bud and flourish so that it yields seed for the sower and bread for the eater, so is my word that goes out from my mouth: It will not return to me empty, but will accomplish what I desire and achieve the purpose for which I sent it."

All the acts performed in the Bible are used to inspire faith and to produce loftier thoughts. Once gained, it teaches you how to navigate and operate your new found abilities. It helps us to navigate by giving us commandments and instructions to follow. As we follow these, our thoughts will benefit because of it.

Genesis 26:5

Because Abraham obeyed me and did everything I required of him, keeping my commands, my decrees and my instructions.

The power we serve wishes to keep us moving in the direction of tomorrow. With this vast overwhelming mystical force that we are given to use, we must accept and heed instruction. Our minds are not equipped to handle such a power. It takes daily guidance from someone skilled in the way to understand it.

Proverbs 3:11-15

My son, do not despise the LORD's discipline, and do not resent his rebuke, because the LORD disciplines those he loves, as a father the son he delights in. Blessed are those who find wisdom, those who gain understanding for she is more profitable than silver and yields better returns than gold. She is more precious than rubies; nothing you desire can compare with her.

We must examine these words as to know ourselves. The difficulties that we face are from a pure lack of understanding. We pass up lofty thoughts to squabble and to think about ordinary things. To concentrate on ourselves will only breed lack and limitations. Just as you used to offer yourselves as slaves to impurity and to ever-increasing wickedness, so now offer yourselves as slaves to righteousness leading to holiness. With this great power we are afforded, we must seek to us it for the betterment of all. The Bible is nothing more than a living, breathing book of thought. Put your time into understanding thought so that you will eventually understand yourself.

Ephesians 5: 8-10

For you were once darkness, but now you are light in the Lord. Live as children of light (for the fruit of the light consists in all goodness, righteousness and truth) and find out what pleases the Lord.

What pleases us doesn't always please the power, but what pleases the power will always please us. The power wants us to live life abundantly on a larger-than-life scale. Man seems to be content with just enough for himself. If you focus on only yourself, that breeds thoughts of limited supply. If you had enough for everyone, you would never be worried about your own meals. Some have others who work for them and they look to squeeze every ounce of work out of the back of the person being paid. If you put a stipulation of working hard in order to receive, then the same stipulation must be put on you. After all, it was you who came up with the idea.

Matthew 7:12-14

So in everything, do to others what you would have them do to you, for this sums up the Law and the Prophets. Enter through the narrow gate. For wide is the gate and broad is the road that leads to destruction, and many enter through it. But small is the gate and narrow the road that leads to life, and only a few find it.

We are all alive, but very few of us are living. Existing is not living. True life, the art of living, is only done and had through the act of pursuit. For we are not seeking to pursue a worthwhile goal; we are merely existing. Nature is always expanding and seeking ways to further life. The art of living can really be seen if you watch water flow on a house. Water seeks to find its level; it will continue to move and to take on new shapes until it has reached a point that it can no longer go. But until this point is reached, it seeks to find escape and doesn't stop until it does. Equate the life of water to us. Let us continue to move, excel and to elevate, only stopping when we are dead. Because when you stop moving, natures assumes you are choosing death. If you don't need the force to move, then you don't need the force at all. Let your conscious be your guide and use your thoughts to elevate yourself as well as others. We must seek to think high thoughts and to understand that great power that we have been given.

2 Timothy 2:15

Do your best to present yourself to God as one approved, a worker who does not need to be ashamed and who correctly handles the word of truth.

Poem: *Chapters*

Who am I? Pages turn in my life
I was once unsure but through pursuit, vision is becoming clearer
I change—could not always feel as I do—will one day not be able to feel as I do now
I change for evolution's sake /I grow /parts of me die /I'm me/
I was alone but changed into a family /caring for those that in a blink of an eye will soon care for me
I've learned to take advantage of my thoughts and not to simply think for thinking's sake
There is power in my pages/ where the end is marked, what I have created will turn so that it is endless!/our story. /Only I close the book! my /I /is the new that touches every/ I /after this
A piece of me to continue in different form—fire never dies /only changes torches/ But burns! My part in creation will continue /I exist/I am story/I am life /I AM

Chapter 17
Becoming a Part

John 3:16

For God so loved the world that he gave his one and only Son, that whoever believes in him shall not perish but have eternal life.

Becoming is the best part of the process. It's the best part because only you will know when the process is complete and when you have become a part of something. I say the journey is the best part because you gradually become aware of your powers on it. At first, even though you study, you will regard somethings as mere coincidences. We have been taught the total opposite of what I state now. Since children, we have been ingrained with the notion that we must fight to be a part. On one hand, we are told that God is our father. In the same breath we are told that we must earn our lineage.

We are told that only years of service and painful efforts will bring about salvation. Yes, that is indeed a way to learn the power you possess. To put yourself in hellish situations and force yourself to think your way out. Or you could choose to believe because it is the absolute truth that this power works. You can choose to believe and start your life off on the stable ground of power/understanding as opposed to the shaky ground of weakness/doubt.

Coincidence and chance occurrences will cease to plague your efforts. As you journey further in study and faith, you will see that there is no such thing as these. All things are as a result of some thought had. People called Jesus Christ the great physician; he was regarded as a doctor. It was said that when one would seek Jesus out to be healed from some affliction, before examining what ailed you he would examine your way of thinking. After he was able to find the thought that was responsible for the condition, he eradicated it and then the disease cleared up. Jesus' approach can be regarded as scientific thinking. When you know the truth and follow the thing in question back to the thought that gave it life, it is all about understanding your thought and then controlling it. If you are able to control your thoughts, you will notice yourself able to do different things that you never could before. This isn't an amazing thing; it is only a side effect of applying scientific thought: you notice your power. Your thought power is only regarded as unamazing because we don't use it. If we were aware of our power and used it, we would truly see how amazing it is.

Superman was an amazing creature because he possessed powers that others did not. But on his home planet of Krypton, he was regular because everyone possessed the same powers he did. When you are aware of the powers you possess, you will be transformed to a super human being, because you are that is what you are! All you need to do to be able to wield this great power is to understand it. Power is a side effect of understanding thought; this is similar to how a pill that cures headaches comes along with a side effect that may cause migraines. Only in the power it will work towards your apparent help, never your hurt. If you reach to attain something and for a short time are apparently denied, it is only because that thing is not for you. Patience will prove your friend in that what you desired will arrive shortly, and it will no doubt be leaps and bounds above that thing you were previously denied.

Scientific thought gives you the ability to first understand and then to use your power. Through this new thought process, you notice and study yourself. You collect data and record your findings. At the end, you are able to do more because you understand more. Of course, in all that you do, it will be a process. According to your faith will your power increase. And according to your faith, will you notice at all.

At first, you won't understand. Everything takes intuition or effort to understand. But when you do, water will be wetter, the grass will be greener and life will become sweeter than you could ever have imagined. You will begin to stop and smell the roses, which will be apparent everywhere. When you become a part, no longer does life live you; you begin to live life. Things begin to go your way. This is like being in heaven; you will have continuous good thoughts. Then your mind and thought process will be changed. You will begin living in a new state of mind.

When you are able to reach this point of clarity, situations that occur are not problems but situations. They will be viewed in a new light; you will be able to step back and view as to get a clearer perspective. When you reach this point, you will no longer see the good and bad in things; you will only see the situation at hand and what should be thought about to extract the greatest results for the whole. When you become a part, you are less anxious to prove your point. After all, what is a point? A point is a vain expression not worth stating. If it is for the whole, its apparent value will soon manifest itself on its own and without your help. When you become aware of this, you will be able to walk away from meaningless situations, because in them you see no benefit for the whole.

When you are a part, you begin to rely on the He that is in me/you rather than the He that is in the world. Both He's are you, and both He's require a life of service. But one regards a life of service to the whole and the other regards a life of service to the self. Either thought process will bring benefits to the whole, but only one process will bring benefits to the part/you! It is up to you.

We were put here to use the power or to be used by the power to effect change. In the midst of this change that is taking place (with or without us), we are afforded dominion over everything. With our power of thought, which is our birthright, we can purposely seek to expand or to propel the expansion of the universe. With proper thought, we will exhibit and manifest the best. But in the process of becoming a part, you begin to subconsciously/automatically think this way. You will begin to think, feel and act the best way regardless of the situation. The outcome will be simply that: an outcome—another situation that will need to be dealt with. Whether you choose to yell, be nice, act a fool or smile, the situation will still play out as it was always supposed to. It is not the situation but how it's dealt with.

The situation is already determined because of the thought that precipitated it. All you do with your reaction to it is give it more life or deter its progression. Either we are in the way or with the way. When you are with the way, all can see the power working in, through and around you. When you are in the way, you resemble something others can clearly see that they do not want to be. They don't know why; they just know that they don't want to be a part. Even when we aren't a part, our spirit attempts to warn us of dangers. When you are not a part, you can recall saying, "I should have followed my first mind." When you are a part, you are your first mind; it followed no different than a crosswalk sign. Your thought seems to navigate you instinctively. You and your inner self are one. No longer do you struggle with yourself; rather, you seek the advice that your inner self is always eager to give. You find yourself on the same page with all of creation, seeking only that council with others that are equally yoked.

The same force that is in and around everything stimulating growth and causing death is in you. You are one with the almighty. You are one with nature and everything that makes up everything else.

Poem: *Anonymously*

I give my secrets anonymously; trust in their authenticity! Save your money and take as many chances as you can while you're young. Invest, put money into making money; remember, millionaires have 6 incomes and billionaires 13. Disregard spending; there will be plenty of time for that. Better to be wealthy than to look rich. Hustle as hard as you can and save; good times won't last always. Prepare for the hard times around the corner as you know that they are on their way. Whatever your grind, go for broke; if you lose, you lose, but when you win, your gamble will be worth more. Springboard into legal business. In business is God; you will learn you. In business you must trust in him, when he is nowhere in sight. In business there are no handouts unless it's proven you don't need one. Through monetary struggle you find God! He is in every part of business. To succeed in business you must believe first in your product then in the market but most of all in yourself; that is the true definition of faith: belief, belief, belief. Learn the rules and spend what it takes to win. Unless you spend, you won't make. Treat your business partners like family; never let anything come between you and a profitable relationship. I say this anonymously because I am the wealthy man who you thought never had a dime. And I'd prefer to keep it that way!

CHAPTER 18
WHAT IS MONEY?

Matthew 25:29

For whoever has will be given more, and they will have an abundance. Whoever does not have, even what they have will be taken from them.

Money is an expression of knowledge or understanding (of your job, of how to sell, of how to do anything that you earn from, even life and how you live it). The word is the tool of thought just as money is the tool of knowledge/power. Money is the seat of importance. But to say money and the word hold more importance than understanding and thought is putting the cart before the horse. This confuses the purpose, which confuses the thought. With money being a tool of knowledge, you begin to see and understand how to use it effectively. Your money is a representation of you, so with money being your representative, you are able to benefit from the good done by it. If you help one person, you are blessed, correct? But if through the power of money you are able to help 100 people, are you not blessed more? Money is a tool that should be used to further our advancement of the kingdom, which is ourselves.

We should use our money to help, because you get that which you give. At first you may only be able to give thought, but that is the biggest gift of all. As you understand, your tangible ability to give will increase. First you will give thought, then your time and then your money. But the first thing will increase the amount of the last thing. As you understand and grow, the last thing will increase the amount of the first thing. It is a never-ending cycle that can only be set in motion and can only be stopped by you. The more you give, the more you receive. So how is money a tool? Money is a tool in that it extends your ability to bless others.

In business, if you can bless a person with a useful product, they will bless you with currency. You will be blessed with currency according to the amount of people you bless with your product. That is why a businessman's spirit instinctively guides him to do more in business. As we bless we get blessed. Money is the tool that can open that doorway up big enough to drive a truck through. I am talking on a spiritual level.

On a worldly level, money is just as big of a tool as on the spiritual level. Why is it then regarded like the end-all be-all? Money is used to make a situation easier like any other tool. And like any other tool, it is to be used when needed. So why is money so highly regarded? It is highly regarded because it is looked at as understanding, not as the tool it is. If I asked you to dig a hole, what tool would you go and get? A shovel of course. What did you use to obtain the shovel? You used money, no doubt. So this then makes money also a tool, but it makes it the ultimate tool. With it you can buy any and all other tools. Regardless of the tools it can purchase, it is still just a tool.

Think of this: You are on a small island whose inhabitants are primitive, with no food or water. The only thing you have is a million cash dollars. Strangely enough, the inhabitants on this island don't recognize money as currency. They only recognize shovels, and you are fresh out. Now understand and see how money is just a tool, and if held in the proper respect, you can use it effectively to gain more tools.

I will tell any and all who hear me: I would never die over a shovel. I would never risk my life for a shovel. As a matter of fact, every shovel I have is in the tool shed with rust and dirt on it. Some are clean but they don't shine like new. To be truly honest, I could care less if they did. To be more honest, I don't ever think about them until it is time to dig a hole. So why do we focus so much on money when it is understanding and knowledge we should seek? The expression "a fool and his money will soon part" sheds light on this. Because in life, getting money is easy; the tricky part is hanging on to it. This part would not be so tricky if we would just seek to know.

We give no thought to retaining money; we only think of ways to make it. But if you make $50 but lose $100 in the process, did you truly profit? Money is elusive to us because we don't study to know it; we just MAKE IT. But we make it to give it away because we have no clue as to how it's kept. I hear so many condemn the practice of tithing, not understanding that tithing is the universe's way of showing you how to save. If you put away ten percent of your money, you will see that it is indeed posing to save. Now if you take this thought of saving even further, you can get even greater use from it. You can easily put 20 percent to savings, 30 percent to rent (saving any extra), 5 percent to entertainment, 30 percent to household and 15 percent to transportation. Or you can break your money up any way that you choose. But do you see where tithing gives you this pathway to saving?

Another reason for tithing is to show faith in the process of the process. Tithing shows that you value the way more than an expression of it. Valuing money more than knowledge is like wanting to talk to Michael Jordan on the phone instead of meeting him in person. Knowledge is the master of money; the more you understand, the more you align yourself to receive. Money must not be loved; find pleasure in knowing the path. Find pleasure in understanding; the more you understand, the more money you will accumulate. I implore you to focus more on understanding because when you gain, you will know how to proceed. Making money is truly only the beginning. You have not arrived just because you have accumulated money. Once money is accumulated, you will be tested as to your ability to keep it and to make more.

Money is a tool and it must be studied to be understood and used properly. You can be your own guide as to your understanding of money by simply asking yourself how much do you have? I'm not asking how much passes through your hands. I'm saying how much money are you able to keep? Do you invest your money to make more money, or do you carelessly spend it adding to another's purse? Money is one of the biggest tools used to inspire greater thought. There is much emotion behind the handling of money. When you save money, you do so with a feeling of attraction. When you invest your money, you do it with a feeling of attraction. Most everything you do with money is followed by a strong emotion. If you give with your heart, you put out a feeling of receiving. Through the law of the universe and the law of attraction, you draw to yourself the equivalent of this thought. But, when you give or pay bills with a feeling of lack or a feeling of having an insufficient supply, you begin to close off your own supply because the universe must match the feeling you have. The universe must honor your intent. Pay the bill with a feeling of pride and a feeling of expectancy. Have pride in the fact that you have been favored. Have pride knowing that out of all the people in the world who can't pay their bills, you can. You can also expect that next month, you will be able to pay the bill with no problem whatsoever. You are able to provide housing, transportation, clothing and food for yourself and for your family.

Every bit of money you have in your pocket should be organized. Say to yourself, "I will attract more." Every time you handle money, say this to yourself as you organize it. You will see that this method will attract more. The only secret to keeping money is studying to know how to. Lastly, love not this tool. Love the help that it can provide. Disrespect not this tool. There are people dying daily for that which you waste, so use it for what it's good for while being careful not to lose your soul.

Matthew 19:23-24

Then Jesus said to his disciples, "Truly I tell you, it is hard for someone who is rich to enter the kingdom of heaven. Again I tell you, it is easier for a camel to go through the eye of a needle than for someone who is rich to enter the kingdom of God."

A rich man's heart no longer needs power. Use money for what it's good for while being careful not to lose your soul. And above all, my brothers and sisters, invest. Follow the laws of the universe and the path set by nature in that everything is used and reused again and again as to get the maximum benefit out of it. But also, as in nature, this is ingeniously done so that in doing so it insures that the supply will never end!

Poem: *Peace Be Still*

Peace be still; let all the negativity swarming cease! I command that the waters of my mind come under my control. I put my hands firmly at the helm of this vessel and I steer. I do not propose to do it alone but I ask that you occupy me. Let your spirit and my mind and body become one, so that you can produce your fruit and let the vines be not broken; manifest through me. Peace be still; let me gain control over me through you. I believe I can; let this mustard seed-like faith be enough as you said it would be. Let this be the power that I need to start this journey of controlling my mind. All I need is to be able to concentrate and to take back myself! In the spirit of doing so, I command my mind: peace be still!

CHAPTER 19
THE MIND STATE'S EFFECTS

Romans 8:7

The mind governed by the flesh is hostile to God; it does not submit to God's law, nor can it do so.

Every thought effects every thought until you have set loose with each thought a chain of events that will lead to a tangible outcome in kind to the thought that set it in motion, just as sure as Sunday follows Saturday. We give life to the inanimate by thought. It will not fizzle out until asked or until its job is complete. You would never ask the helpful to leave, so only the unhelpful thought must be respectfully disregarded. I say respectfully as to give proper respect to thoughts so they can be taken seriously.

Every deed or word was precipitated by a thought. No thought is big or small because the tiny snowball once set loose to roll down the hill will gain speed, force and size to eventually resemble any size imagined. So all thought must be respected. After you can respect your thoughts, your thoughts will respect you. When your thoughts are respected, the firmness of will can be applied because you are finally aware of the power of thought. We now give respect only to action, but the true power lies in the thought behind it. After you have had so many kinds of similar thoughts, it develops itself into process. Once a thought process has been created, it no longer needs you to actively participate. This thought process will produce unto its kind until you change it. The original thought is like the tree and all the other thoughts that follow are first the roots then the branches then the leaves, which can number into the millions. It will produce unto its kind. Soon you will have an orchard of thoughts you don't want.

These thoughts that you don't want will in time develop into things you don't want. Your thoughts are you most powerful allies or your worst enemies. Set them free with your attitude towards others and towards life. The golden rule, "Do unto others as you would have done to you," pertains to the thought you set free. You will begin to only think the grand as opposed to the arbitrary. That saves you; that elevates you. The thoughts that you think for others are the thoughts that you entertain. If they be lofty, you will think so for others; if you will think so for others, it will be the same for yourself. You can't serve two masters: either your thoughts will be lofty or they will be regular. Either you lean on love or you harbor hate. We have both thoughts but nature is not neutral. Things are either living or dying. There is no stationary to life; you can't momentarily have a thought without it producing that unto its kind. Those thoughts you wish to retract, only ask and it will be done.

The universe follows your thoughts. It cannot be fooled, tricked or deceived. It will give you what you are asking for, just as you ask for it. Watch what you wish for; you just might get it. Know what you are asking for because it is on the way. Understand that the thoughts you have are the brick and mortar to the things that will manifest. If you practice larceny, you will receive that unto its kind. Examine your life and be honest in that all you live, you thought. Pause and take the time to analyze your yesterdays. Do they not reflect exactly the thoughts you entertained at the time? This may appear scary at first, and rightly so because it means that you have power, control and dominion over you. Well, you do and your yesterdays are truly on your shoulders. Whether pleasing or not, all the things that have transpired, you precipitated by thought.

At first, it may be overwhelming, but then you will regard it as the greatest gift. Once trained, your thoughts will correspond to your mind like a seasoned elephant in a circus show. When you can't breathe, you notice breathing; when you can't swallow, you notice your throat, but until then they went as unnoticed as last week's morning coffee. It becomes habit. After time, it will be as common as breathing. At first you will seek blessings, but as you realize and become one, blessings will in turn seek you.

Acquiring faith is like pushing a small snowball up a big hill. At first it is easy; at first it is something to shout about because it is so simple, but the more you journey, the bigger the ball gets until finally the faith you push appears to be pushing back. This is the test: How badly do you want to know? How badly do you want to reach the top? It appears difficult, and it is; let's not forget you are pushing a huge snowball up a hill. Truly understand that the harder it is, it can only mean one thing: You are nearing the top. That last push to get it to the peak may be the greatest challenge yet. But understand nature: It is inevitable that what goes up must come down.

You have worked tirelessly pushing and wrestling to understand with your faith to get it to this point. You feel out of breath and overworked. Nature is now in control in the form of gravity. The ball you pushed up now begins to slowly roll down. The faith you endured to understand now is in control on its own. Your universe wants to show you and reward you for the level of understanding you have achieved. Your belief, your faith, and your thought is rewarded unto its kind! So your faith now roles slowly at first; then you must jog to keep up; then you must run. You are no longer in stride; your faith, your level of understanding and your thought begins to precede you. You are in spirit and no longer find yourself needing to be told to help, to give or to contribute your time. As those lofty thoughts bear fruit unto their kind, you no longer find yourself entertaining fear, poverty or weakness of any sort. Your thoughts carry you to a place you could have never dreamed of, whether they be lofty or the opposite. Your thoughts are the boat in which you will travel to your destination. Wherever it is can only be attributed to the one thinking the thoughts

Poem: *Eventually*

I'm going to make it all the way so blessed and highly favored that you will not be able to deny me. As the cosmos and all it has to offer unfolds and finds an exit through my form. Expression is my nature; I am as flawless as birth! Able to understand the riddles of time by sheer intuition. Eventually, you will see. Eventually, it will come full circle. As I rise, my mental only grows. Help is on the way. Eventually, we will understand that God is in and not up, able to be talked to at will as he is omnipotent. A piece of me is always with him. As he is omnipresent, a piece of him is always with me. Eventually, we will teach our children to understand that greater is he that is in me than thee that is within the world. Mathematics is very important but an understanding of the piece of God you share with all of creation is of far greater consequence. Eventually is on its way!

Chapter 20

In the Power of Thought He Will Never Leave or Forsake You

Deuteronomy 31:6

Be strong and courageous. Do not be afraid or terrified because of them, for the LORD your God goes with you; he will never leave you nor forsake you.

If the power of I AM lies in our ability to think, I think therefore I AM. If I Am is the power itself and it is in us in our ability to think, and it's a proven fact that we constantly think, whether asleep or awake, then the power is constantly with us and shall never leave or forsake. Be strong and courageous enough to think positively.

Don't be afraid when you have negative thoughts, because he is always with us, and he will never leave or forsake. You have control to command and to lead your thoughts. The power, no matter what, is always present, and it is always with us because we cannot stop thinking. Don't be afraid to think; step up your thoughts, and think those things that will bring you pleasure, not pain! We are able and we should be confident; we should plan courageously and execute fearlessly. No matter what we are afforded a power that will prevail, a power that will deliver us. We are afforded the power of thought, and thought is the biggest power in the cosmos.

Thought is always there producing fruit unto its kind. If what you have received isn't what you wanted, the power isn't leaving or forsaking you. It is taking you at your thought and giving that which you asked for. Because it/the power knows that you have sense enough to never think the things into existence that you don't want. Or do we?

We always want to look up and ask God why, but try looking into the mirror and asking the person you see. Why do you keep asking for that which you don't want? You think all day, every day, and the power is all day, every day granting that which you say you want, which is what you think. When you fall asleep, that is when the real work begins. Your subconscious takes over when you sleep and it gets to work; you see results. It diligently attracts those things to you that you say you want. The power has no concept of good or bad and right or wrong because those things don't exist. It only sees what you think about which in turn is that which you want. It brings these things no matter what they are to us for our benefit. Whether we have thought through our request or our prayer or not, it brings us that which we think about. It brings it to us by using the positive power of the mind to cause effect on electrons; this is the part of the power in which you are granted dominion.

Your subconscious acts upon your thoughts, which in turn begin to move on neutrons to form atoms. The atoms come together to produce matter, and matter makes up everything that you see. That is the way that our dominion works, by our positive thought particles which are a part of everything in the form of electrons. Electrons are the base particles that are in everything. So, you are in everything and everything is in you. We are a part of the vine. Our power is in thought; our power is in the knowledge and the acknowledgement of our birthright and the ability to think. You have the power regardless if you know it or not. It has nothing to do with you accepting a certain God or a certain religion. But if you are ignorant to the power inside of you, it will lead you to say things like, "I feel so alone" or "It's me against the world." Those are the statements of the truly blind. How can you/we/me ever be alone if everything we are makes up everything we see?

You aren't wrong, stupid or anything like that. I just point out this great truth because without this knowledge, you suffer and you do so needlessly. We suffer because we put ourselves to the left and our thoughts on the right. Or better and more simply put, we put God in the sky and we are on the ground. When in all actuality, God is in the temple along with me as one at the top. The temple is in our brain where inside lies the ability to think, to commune and to be one with God—to connect! What we don't understand is that the connection is the reception of that which you wish. It could be knowledge, money, health, love, or anything the mind can come up with. You know for a fact that he will never leave or forsake because you will never stop thinking; you are incapable of it as he is incapable of ever leaving or forsaking you. As long as you can think, you GOT GOD!

What should this mean to us? It should mean that we are confident in our abilities, not in our physical possessions. Why fall in love with the possession? Instead, you should fall in love with the thing that acquired it: your ability to think! Recognize your power, so that you can be set free. Be set free from fear of any kind, lack and limitation. Be set free from thought that seeks to kill, steal and destroy your dreams, your imagination and your ability to think. The only way to lose it is to give it away, because it can't be taken. The only way to give it away is by keeping a closed mind. All we must do to gain this liberty and understanding is to acknowledge the fact that GREATER IS HE THAT IS IN ME THAN HE THAT IS IN THE WORLD! Once this is done, you gain a level of confidence that will give you the power to start controlling your thoughts. The only power it gives is the power of knowledge and the power to understand that you can. You can control your thoughts just as sure as you can control your actions. The time it takes to understand this great truth will differ for us all. But by your level of faith will your timetable be determined. It is no race, because once gained, it will feel as if it was always there.

Once recognized, you will understand why there is no other gift that can match the power of thought.

We have been given the actual keys to the kingdom. What will you do with your set? The power is us; a new batch of thought is created with the frequency that every breath is taken, and that still doesn't match the rates that thought is had by. The supply is infinite and it is as vast as the possibilities of thought combinations able to be created by man. There is nothing new under the sun, but we can change and adjust the combinations that we put together. If we do that, we can produce/create new things. That is what is meant by infinite power.

Everything, like anything, is a challenge to learn at first. Since all is in thought, there will be some naturals. As you do push-ups, your stamina will increase. Over time, you will be able to do more. As your abilities increase, so shall your strength. Strength is a byproduct of exercise. Stronger thought and clearer thought is a byproduct of scientific thought. As you continue to do it, it will get easier, until at last, thought takes over, proving that he will never leave or forsake you. In the end, the power appears to be keeping you, being that protective hedge against all things.

At the center of your hedge is your ability to deal with things in a new way. No longer do you lose control. In chaos you will come alive; you will know true peace in thought and be able to walk the stormy seas of your mind at will. Peace be still. Nothing is out of reach when this level of inner self is attained. When this level of peace is attained, you concretely know it. ALL IS POSSIBLE. The man whose reach is not long enough to grasp that which he desires is the man who says his reach is not long enough. We all know that for him to say his reach wasn't long enough, he thought his reach wasn't long enough. AND THAT MAKES IT TRUE! Only for him, however, and only for those blind enough to follow his truth!

ABOUT THE AUTHOR

My name is David Allen Wright, I was born in Cleveland, Ohio, in 1973 to Mr. Charles and Virginia Wright. My upbringing was in the church, but like many children do, I strayed from what I was taught. I thought that in life I knew it all and set out to prove it. The life that I lived up until these 43 years has only been what I made of it. Good, bad, or indifferent, I made these choices myself. I got into trouble following what I knew to the wrong way. Of course, I had ups and downs, more downs than ups. I learned a lot along the way but mostly I learned this great truth: that our thoughts are the things that create what we have in life. We, as everyday humans, have the power to reach deep inside our minds and dare to be HAPPY. We have the power to produce in thought all that we wish and see in our minds. My mother would always tell me as a child, "Don't let anyone steal your dreams." I learned that that meant to think freely. As long as you have the courage and strength to think for yourself, every dream you dream can be attained. If you would only live a life based on controlling your thoughts. You would see that heaven isn't so far away.

To learn more about David and his books, please visit his website at www.thinkforyourself.life.